The Little Book of Crypto

Preamble

Welcome to the Little Book of Crypto. This book has been written for those of you looking to get an honest introduction into the world of cryptocurrency. Or, as I like to say a no BS approach to an introduction.

This book is for everyone who wants to find an enjoyable entry into the crypto world. Please take it on its face, you may not agree with everything that's written in here, but I encourage you to enjoy it nonetheless. Remember, nothing in here should be taken as legal or financial advice of any kind. It's all designed to be recreational.

Dedication is paid to everyone working in the industry. The knights who are trying to shape its future and those who have spent countless hours innovating in the hope that it becomes the daily norm.

-First published 2019-

Legals

This book and its contents are copyright subject to US Copyright laws. Copyright filed with the U.S. Copyright office Case # 1-8163176811. No part or parts of this book maybe copied or reproduced without the express written consent of the author.

Nothing written in this book is designed to be legal, financial, or investment advice of any kind. Any reference to persons or people is made only in a speculative nature and is designed to be educational in nature. Additionally information about persons or people is designed to amount to journalistic writing. Any mention of any cryptocurrency or company in this book is not a claim of association or endorsement. Some trademarked items maybe referenced in this book. Those trademark belong to the respective trademark holders and nothing in this book should be taken as a claim or endorsement of those trademarks.

Digital Ebook ISBN: 978-1-79232259-4

Print ISBN 978-1-7923-2288-4

Contents

Chapter 1 - Intro.
Chapter 2 - The Law?
Chapter 3 - Types of Crypto
Chapter 4 - The Cryptographic Sale
Chapter 5 - Bulls and Bears
Chapter 6 - Mining and Wallets
Chapter 7 - The Future

Chapter 1 - Intro

How do you start a book about Cryptocurrencies?

This is the question I pondered for literally weeks... Well, months. I never believed that writer's block could be a real thing, but there I was. I would sit looking at my laptop, and it would just be there, looking right back at me. No matter how hard I tried, I just could not get words to appear on the page in some kind of order that I truly liked.

I spent months going back and forth like this. It got to the point where people began to wonder if I was actually serious about writing a book. Perhaps this was just another stupid idea I had come up with in my head. The real problem was not writing words; that bit was easy. I wrote maybe eight different versions of the first chapter.

The Little Book of Crypto

Ok, more like 10. The only problem was that I wanted the book to be honest, and no matter how hard I tried I couldn't get the honesty to come across. At least not in a way that I felt people would understand what I was trying to say.

In order to understand what other people had written, I picked up a number of other Cryptocurrency books and managed to read through them with ease. A real simple read for those who are looking for a great 101 on cryptocurrencies. Now, as easy and well written as they may have been, this was not what I wanted to achieve. True, I wanted to write an introduction to Cryptocurrencies, but not in a textbook, classroom, stuck up your ass kind of way. My aim in writing a Cryptocurrency book was not to tell people, in idiotic terms, what Cryptocurrencies are and what they do. My plan was to get an

Chapter 1 - Intro

honest book into the market, to talk to people about what Cryptocurrencies really are and what they really do. How they impact people, business, governments and leave a footprint like no other technology has left before. Something, which for some reason, no one had ever bothered to do before.

You see, Cryptocurrencies aren't just a FAD or a phase like some other technologies. They are a new generation of technologies that are designed to change the way we do many, so many, of our day to day things. They have a following, a community. They build projects, solve problems, and scare the crap out of the establishment. These are just some of the many reasons so many people love them with passion. I can't think of another technology since the internet that came along with this much power. None of these attributes is over

The Little Book of Crypto

exaggerated or made up in any capacity.

For that reason I am going to introduce you to Cryptocurrencies in a way, I think, has never been done before, in a literarily sense. I am going to give you an 'insiders' view into the Cryptocurrency market: how things work, what people do and what you need to look for when you enter and start out within it.

You see, Cryptocurrencies are becoming the norm and if you start to adapt now, you will find yourself ahead of the curve. Very much ahead. And let me assure you that the people who made money in the .com bubble (or any other kind of major industry shift) were all in the industry ahead of the curve. Although it may seem like I am portraying Cryptocurrencies as this amazing new thing (which I think it is) I

Chapter 1 - Intro

am not saying it is a revolutionary new technology which will solve every problem known to man. I am also not saying it is saintly. Is there a dark side to cryptocurrencies? Yes. However, are there awesome stories to be told? Yes, too.

I am sure that there are those within the industry who may disagree a little with what I say. There are also those who may agree with it completely. The only thing I can do is share my opinions and views on some key things in the hope that in doing so, I can help you understand the cryptocurrency industry a little bit more. Not just in some 101 view that is going to make you run out and buy a bunch of Bitcoin, but the type of understanding that will make you fall in love with it like I did. The only real way I know how to do that is to be totally honest with you, so through the duration of this book I am going to do something very few books do: I am going to treat you like an adult. A fully grown mature adult. I will give you the best introductory guide I can produce, for you to walk you into the industry head-on. No hand holding, no bullshit. Just raw information that will give you the kind of education everyone needs in an industry which is growing as fast as the cryptocurrency industry is.

With all of that in mind, we're about to walk through the journey that is cryptocurrency together. So, sit tight.

Housekeeping
The first thing you need to understand is that there are some phrases and principals you are going to have to get to know in order for me to educate you as fast as I can. With that in mind, you need to digest and learn the following before we go any further:

Chapter 1 - Intro

No one actually calls it 'Cryptocurrency' - It is just 'Crypto'. Like many other technologies things get abbreviated and I want to talk to you like an adult; to do that, I'm not using its full industry term name like a child that's in trouble with his mother.

'Crypto' is a term that is given to any kind of token or coin within the industry. Basically, a cryptographic token (Cryptocurrency) in any form. Later we are going to look at a breakdown for different types of currencies and the different things they do. I will walk you through these more in depth. However, for now you need to know that even if someone calls their coin a 'coin' or a 'token' it still is, essentially, a cryptocurrency and therefore we call it a crypto. As a quick reference point, these can be Altcoins, Legacy Coins, Security Tokens, Utility Tokens, or Shitcoins.

The Little Book of Crypto

At no time should you think of anything in this book as an investment, financial, or legal advice. Everything in this book is designed to be educational; more of an introduction to the subject. Not a set of hard and fast rules as to what you should do and how you should do it. If you're looking for that kind of education you've come to the wrong place!

There are other coins outside of Bitcoin. By now there are actually hundreds if not thousands of coins within the industry. All linked to a different project and all serving a different purpose. If you think Crypto is just Bitcoin, you are in for a serious surprise. The industry has grown up so much since Bitcoin, and if anyone says to you Cryptocurrency is just Bitcoin, they are talking total crap.

The Crypto industry is not made up of JUST Coins. The industry has grown so

Chapter 1 - Intro

much that it is now made up of different segments within it, including: Crypto media, Crypto marketing, development firms, mining firms, financial firms, exchanges, market places, and many others. There is a whole genuine industry that revolves around crypto. So when you think of crypto, don't think of just some guys sitting at their computers exchanging Bitcoins with each other. Everything has grown up a lot since then. Just to give you an idea on how big the industry is at the moment: last year the largest crypto exchange made more money than Deutsche bank.

FYI, Cryptography is a type of maths. Thats where the word Crypto comes from.

It's called Cryptocurrency because it uses cryptographic equations to confirm and verify the transactions

The Little Book of Crypto

which take place.

Everyone in this industry calls themselves an expert. However, the industry is nowhere near old enough for anyone to be an 'expert'. Those guys you see on CNN or BBC are full of shit. Three years ago they were working in a totally different field doing something totally different. Next year, they will still be doing something different. So, since this industry is so new, the only way you can know for certain is by doing your own research. There is some exceptions to this and there are some great people working within the industry. However, you should always assume that everyone you are speaking with is talking utter BS. If you want to learn more from someone or get some advice, learn more about them before you learn about what they say. The advantage for a con-person of this being such a new industry is that it is

Chapter 1 - Intro

difficult to fact check. Take an old school approach to everyone you meet; be serious about them.

I hate lawyers who work in the Crypto space. Don't ask me why, I just do. I play nice with other lawyers and have nothing but respect for them. However, there's a difference between a Crypto lawyer and a lawyer that works in crypto. I'm the former. It's as if a car mechanic who also fixes bikes, buses, and boats wants to sit there and tell you they're an expert at fixing cars. It just doesn't work like that. Also, when a lawyer tells you that they are rated by an 'in industry' rating system such as Chambers and Partners or some other law rating system, it's bullshit. There's no sore feeling here, believe me, however how are guys sitting at the rating agencies able to compare top litigators, mediators, and then crypto lawyers? They're not. They have no idea of the challenges the industry faces, so work with lawyers that already work in the industry. The amount of problems I have had to clean up from lawyers, even from big firms, who have no idea of what they are doing, is outstanding. Just because you are paying more money does not mean you are getting a better service when it comes to crypto.

The Origin Story
In terms of an origin story there's not many that are better than Crypto. If you read a traditional book on the subject they skip over the real and most important stuff. Or give you a half hearted version. That's actually fair as I don't believe that anyone has the full story; however, we should touch on it so that you at least have a basic understanding.

There isn't a much cooler origin story than Crypto. The reality is that Crypto

Chapter 1 - Intro

was invented by a person or group of people unknown. Honestly, we have no idea who created Crypto. Most of the people who claim or are known to have had a hand in creating Bitcoin are dead. What is actually mind blowing is this: Crypto is a number of different technologies that are married together to create one overall technology. No patents filed. No money grabbed. A stranger stepped out into the world and said, here guys, have these. I haven't seen anything that cool since the doctor who created the Polio vaccine explained in an interview that a vaccine belonged to the people, and that the concept of patenting was unconscionable. A pioneer with a love for his industry. I believe that is exactly what happened here as well.

In fact, some of these technologies are actually revolutionary. I call them pioneering technologies; this means there has been nothing like them before they were created. They didn't update existing technology and they didn't remold something that already existed. They were created from scratch. If someone was to patent them, they would be a millionaire. Well, probably a billionaire.

Coming back to the origin story, what we do know about it is scattered. The underlying belief is that it was created by a person, or a group of people, who called themselves Satoshi Nakamodo. Over the last few years there's been people who have suggested that 'they' created it and are Satoshi… Needless to say, no one has actually proved it.

There have been a few who have suggested they are Satoshi. We call these people Faketoshis'. Some have even gone so far as to fill patents and law suits to prove the point -none of

Chapter 1 - Intro

which have been successful. Every few months, someone pops up to claim that they are the creator of Bitcoin, but fall on their face to explain basic facts. The guys who have gone to court have failed to prove anything as well, and in fact, after reading the transcripts of depositions taken from some who claim to be Satoshi, and twinning that with judgements on the subject, it blows my mind how some of these idiots can make the claims they do and believe that they can get away with it. Especially when they lie to a court. Yes, indeed you can usually tell when someone is full of crap. Not only can't they prove anything but their followers will often attack people who disagree with that assertion, even if something is simply subjectively written about that particular individual and simply stating facts.

And as a side note, when I wonder how we can elect idiots into positions of power over the political spectrum across the world, and then I see how some of these people react to objectively written articles, I begin to understand. The "don't believe my viewpoint and I will shoot you down" has become the new norm for these folks. It's going to be a hard day when the things they believe in are debunked and their views are shown to be as radical as they are.

The reality is that someone gave away masses of technology for free, so it seems slightly contradictory that his or her biggest followers would be attacking people who disagree with this view point. It is also worth noting that some of these Faketoshis' have created their own coin, with a project, team, and goals (often to get rich) behind it. The feeling by many is that they will simply

Chapter 1 - Intro

make outrageous claims, file law suits, patents, etc. to promote their own coin, in the hope of driving the price up. Oh, and with the type of followers we see for this kind of people, any criticism of their coin, mining, or any element associated with it meets with harsh resistance. When Faketoshis' do things that are outside of the spirit of Crypto and the community that lives within it, it is hard to believe someone would act so generous and then suddenly turn on the industry they created. Much like a mother abandoning its child. Those actions alone get many hatred from within the industry. Even by those who simply try and stay objective.

Only time will tell if the real creator wants to admit to who they are, but for now there has been no cast iron evidence of one single creator. We know that some people have had a hand in creating Bitcoin; that much was evidenced.

I am sure that more people will pop up claiming to be the 'founder and creator' of crypto, though. Even on a second review of this chapter before editing there is someone new who has come out this week. The reality is that whoever made it did a damn good job of making sure that they could not be discovered. My feeling is that they will aim at keeping it that way. The most valid point is that someone wanting to keep their identity secret makes actually a lot of sense. If you create a technology which essentially shifts the landscape of how money is used between people, has the potential to mess with governments, and undermines the whole banking structure, it would be wise to stay well hidden.

However, those who have actually made

Chapter 1 - Intro

their identity known, seem to have died within the last decade.

Although that may seem suspect, we have to remember that bitcoin was launched ten years ago. Which means its creation was much longer in the making. This is something spoken about within the community, so if only to put curiosity to rest, it would be worth analyzing what actually happened to them briefly, because indeed, it is fair to say that a lot can happen within thirteen years.

When we peel away the onion, there are a few things that marry up. First of all, keeping identity secret is very much in the spirit of crypto. This is so because crypto is decentralized, which means that in its true form no one person, company, or government owns it. If someone admitted or claimed to be the founder, it would undermine the whole

The Little Book of Crypto

belief that Crypto at its core belongs to the people and not to one person or group of people.. Identifying the founder would give a face to the project, and precisely a face, sadly, attracts the worst in people including lawsuits, racial profiling, dislike, and media attention. This person's life would never be the same again. Not to mention the legal ramifications of putting Bitcoin into the jurisdiction of the creator. For example, if the creator were English, it would logically put its origins under English law. Not good for everyone.

Furthermore, if you think about what Bitcoin and crypto does, putting your face to it would very much be a suicidal move. Think of it logically: if you have just created a technology which on its full deployment would and could kill the current banking structure, I wouldn't want my face all over it. I am aware I am repeating what I have said before, but

Chapter 1 - Intro

on a serious note, people have disappeared for much less. There would only be a small window of time before every bank in the world would put you on top of their hit list.

Before you think that's an insane notion, remember that banks control the flow of funds around the globe, so if you are about to disrupt what they do and how they do it, you are literally attacking the biggest institution that exists globally. They help elect presidents, they control funds, and they are now so big that no government in the world can allow them to fail. If you are about to 'kill' them, it would be good idea to maybe not show your face.

Regardless of how much or if you believe at all in any kind of 'deep state' structure, Crypto manages to displace a large amount of the control that governments and banks have over people: by removing their ability to control the economy and financial world, you strip away a huge amount of their power. At a global scale, even just losing the ability to track money will have a massive social and economical impact on the power banks. Twin that with governments' ability to print and control funds within their country. Money, as we know, is the sole reason the government survives. Easily put: you pay funds and the government administers them through, depending on where you are based; it provides services which work for you and them. What we have here, then, is a technology that is so disruptive that it even threatens to change the shape of financial transactions forever. Do you think that such a creation is going to be embraced by the financial, political, and media world?

Chapter 1 - Intro

To put this into context, let's take a real life example. If people stopped using banks because they only used crypto on a peer to peer (person to person) basis, how would the government be able to tax people on their income? How would the government be able to track transactions if they are unmemorable and unidentifiable? How would governments be able to manage the application of funds within their jurisdiction by deploying measures such as quantitative easing? They simply couldn't. Sure, you could be taxed at the source when you were paid, but every other dollar you made outside of work would be yours. The very things that make crypto so powerful are the reason why Bitcoin (and crypto) is shunned and hated by so many of the biggest players.

I left my wallet at home
Crypto uses a wallet principal. This

means that the funds don't have to be stored in a bank like conventional money.

Basically put, what happens every time you use your credit or debit card is the following: the store you want to buy something from has you put your card in a machine, and the purpose of that machine is to do two things: (1) Confirm that you are who you say you are and (2) confirm that you have the funds you claim to have. In that moment, that is all the store cares about. When you enter your PIN or sign a receipt, you prove you are you. The small box then asks about your financial institution: 'does this person have the money to pay'; if the answer is yes, the transaction is authorized. Sometimes that money may go instantly, other times it may take a few days. Either way, both your bank and the provider of that small box will take a small fee for what they have

Chapter 1 - Intro

done. In the moment the bank says 'yes, this person has the funds', they are acting as an 'oracle'. They are confirming that a transaction is verified. With crypto, instead, this 'oracle' is not the bank, but any person who is with the network. Sometimes, we call these nodes.

I promised I wouldn't give you a 101 guide on crypto and I will not.. The purpose of this section is just to explain that if the banks lose the ability to handle your funds, they lose the usefulness of the ability to process transactions.

Banks, in a Crypto world, are simply not needed. If you don't need to keep your funds in a bank and they don't need to be part of your transactions, why would they need to exist? Crypto scares the crap out of banks, it really does. It's like introducing the motorcar to the horse.

The Little Book of Crypto

As a consequence, 98% of Crypto projects that ran throughout 2017 - 2019 could not get any kind of bank account at all. Nothing. Nudda. Most credit card companies actually stopped allowing users to buy crypto from exchanges or brokers. Think of it. Your bank, stopped you from spending YOUR money. Crypto companies couldn't get accounts even if they did nothing but acted as a media company to crypto firms. If the name Crypto or Cryptocurrency was found in the name, you hit a black list. The same is still true today. Most banks will not, under any circumstance, give bank accounts to companies which engage in, create, or work with companies in the crypto space. If that doesn't tell you all you need to know then nothing will. The banks are doing everything they can to stop companies from working within the space, in some kind of politically charged, gate keeper mentality. The job

Chapter 1 - Intro

of the banks is to work for us, not tell us what we can and cannot do with our funds.

On the other hand, sadly, those banks that would and do allow companies in the crypto industry to set up bank accounts, are not the most 'straight' banks. This doesn't mean they don't provide banking facilities, but the reality is that if they were suddenly not in business tomorrow, I don't think too many people would be shocked. On top of that, these banks that by providing accounts do or did allow crypto companies to operate within them, would place the strictest requirements on them and would often be in places where if anything went wrong, there was very little recourse. Their complaints procedure wasn't exactly fair.

Now, it is true that Bitcoin had a bad name to begin with, during the 'dark web days'. This was the period where only those who used the dark web were actually using Bitcoin as a method of exchange. By the way, if you don't know what the dark web is, just imagine the internet with zero rules or accountability. This deployment of Bitcoin across the dark web was the sold excuse banks used for stopping people from buying crypto with their services. There were tails of guys buying pizza and drugs over the internet that involved some kind of weird exchange between people. Folks, the first rule of life is that wherever there is money, there is bad guys. That's a sad fact. And the early days of crypto were very much surrounded in the bad guys' area, through websites such as 'silk road' and used by people to purchase things that none could or would need. You have to remember, though: not EVERY transaction happening at that time was used for illegal or illicit

Chapter 1 - Intro

purposes.

The reality of the situation today is that most financial institutions are shunning crypto while working to actually buy and trade it like a commodity. Some of the largest pension firms and financial institutions on the planet have Bitcoin and other crypto trading desks. When a market can make 4-8% in a day, there is no way that the financial world is going to ignore that. what this means is that in a full sense of messed up logic, banks are playing with the thing which will one day kill them (if they don't adapt). So to put that into a day to day reality, the retail market is not providing banking facilities for something which the trading market is actively working in.

If you think that's insane, wait until you read the next chapters on the law.

The good, the bad, and the dead

The Little Book of Crypto

As I said before, most of the 'creators' or those who have identified themselves as being connected with the original project have died. It would be a shame if we didn't mention that in at least some kind of detail. Like a dirty secret, this is very rarely spoken about except within the crypto sphere where people will occasionally ask the question and wonder if everything is as it is reported.

We know that during the creation of bitcoin there was a period where a number of people were emailing each other deliberating and understanding how Bitcoin would take shape. They were contacted by someone called Satoshi Nakomota, who after some communication and sharing of documents and ideas, went quiet and handed the project off to the group. This was, in essence, a group of experts in a number of fields working on something a stranger had introduced

Chapter 1 - Intro

them too.

The main people who have identified themselves as having something to do with the creation of Bitcoin are numerous. There are those who have tangible proof and those who have just jumped on the bandwagon. We see this all the time: where there is success or tragedy there is also those who claim to be part of it.

Because no-one REALLY knows what happened or who the creator is, I don't want to spend more time than necessary on this. Otherwise, it becomes all about conjuncture and theory. There is a great story here, though, which has been told many times, and there are a few TV documentaries which are actually very informative. For now, I want to keep specifics and facts in your head.

The Little Book of Crypto

About me
So, we hit that bit of the book where I have to introduce myself. While I am keen for you to know who I am and why I am writing this book, I also want you to understand that nothing here amounts to me showing off. There is nothing I hate more than someone downloading on an unsuspecting individual, exactly who they are and what they do, for the purpose of doing some good old fashioned dick measuring (excuse the expression).

What I want to do, though, is tell you my story as more of an inspiration than a justification as to why I am writing this book. In doing so I hope you will understand why I chose to write this book.

I'm a lawyer.

I know what you're thinking.

The Little Book of Crypto

Don't think that.

I graduated from law school in England and have worked in Europe, North America, and the Middle East. I'm a lawyer in a few different countries. However, I hate court rooms and I have always been a tech geek; I paid a lot of my way through university rebuilding old PC's that I would buy online and then flip them for a profit. Windows 10 was a hit at the time; PC's sold at inflated prices if they had it. I had a bootlegged version that I downloaded from a file sharing platform and flipped the PC's I had with that version on it. Full disclosure, with some kind of irony, I am actually sitting at Microsoft's headquarters in Seattle writing this, laughing to myself inside. If only they knew. Bill, I'm sorry, I had bills to pay. I owe you a coffee. The good news is, think of all the adopters of Windows technology there was!

The Little Book of Crypto

I loved gaming. First person shooters mostly. No, not Call of Duty, I'm older than that, Counter Strike 1.4. built rigs, and did some low level coding whenever the mood would suit me. Java, if you are interested. If I actually had more money when I was a student, I would have probably filed a few patents. But, what can I say, 'what if's' never made anyone anything except unhappy. And believe me when I say that during my time as a student there were a bunch of things that now I often wonder: why did I do them? Never with regret, just more 'were you thinking that, really?' So filing patents is pretty much at the bottom of the list.

Truth of it is that I actually only went to university to follow a girl. I was young and in love. Her mom was an absolute saint and helped me through the process to get into university. The girl and I picked similar/same universities

Chapter 1 - Intro

with the hope of going together, but the only problem was that when push came to shove, she picked differently and decided she wanted to go single. I wrestled with even going at all, and actually, I am 99% sure she doesn't know this but: if she wouldn't have gone with me on the first day, chances are I wouldn't have gone at all.

Oh, one last thing. My 6th form (junior college) law professor told me I would never make anything of myself in law; that I should drop out of her class. True story. I guess I proved her wrong?

Today I enjoy much more grown up stuff. I still game, I still design rigs, only now I have to do other stuff like exercise, work, and shop for groceries. The kind of stuff which makes me wonder at what point did I actually become an adult. Or if I even did? Maybe I'm still in my dorm room in the first year of university, asleep. Missing my first class. Maybe this is all a dream? No, wait. I pay taxes, even I'm not weird enough to have an "awesome" life where I pay taxes.

I started my firm, Gresham International, a few years ago. I had moved back to England from California for a number of reasons. My mother was dying, I was getting a divorce, the law firm I was working for had broken down, and I was broke. Stone broke. I used $800 of the last $1800 in my bank account to book my flight back. I decided I had to start my own firm to suit my lifestyle. Not the 'drive fast cars and hardly work' lifestyle, but the one which meant that I could spend more time with my dying mother while getting through a divorce kind of lifestyle. I started by grabbing whatever clients I could, helping them with minor legal issues such as contracts. Lawyers in England don't

Chapter 1 - Intro

make as much as other places, so my best month was when I managed to make $1,000 so I could pay my rent.. I had some friends helping me out, I would be lying if I said I didn't, yet things seemed bleak, even though I had those who cared about me. Unless anyone has ever been there, you will never truly know how much giving someone even a $200 contract can really help them out. There is a plug here: use the smaller firms over the bigger ones, because it will have a better and bigger impact.

Just before I moved back to the UK I had discovered Crypto; Bitcoin and some others that were in the pipeline. I instantly fell in love with it. I was far away from being able to buy any, and mining was something I couldn't afford the equipment for, so I just simply watched the industry. I am one of those rare people who actually admits that I never had any Bitcoin when it was cheap. The truth of it is, even if I did have some, I was so broke I would have sold it at around the $200 - $400 mark to get some cash out. The long game was not in my future.

Being a smaller firm, I aligned with startups very well. I had worked with startups before when I was in London so I understood the challenges and problems that they faced. Startups have always resonated with me as my father was very entrepreneurial. Twinned with the smaller fee structure, it was a marriage that suited well. Hard work, harder times, and honest transactions were all things that resonated with me. So, it became the logical ethos that I (and as the company grew, we) should sever startups and assist those who are at the forefront of new technologies. That idea was abandoned after two weeks.

Chapter 1 - Intro

I ran into my first serious crypto client and, as a result, decided to go full steam ahead into that industry. I had something which so few people have: an opportunity to work with what I knew and loved, all at the same time, so I grabbed it. Admittedly, everyone said I was crazy focusing on an industry that would go nowhere. Today, we are regarded as the largest independent crypto only law firm on the planet, and I'm regarded as one of the best Crypto lawyers. Not the one sitting in some massive firm running their "blockchain team' not giving a crap. Or worse still, not the one who only passed the NY two day bar exam and then called himself a Crypto lawyer. I'm proud of every client we have served, each one we helped build from the ground up, and all those who have supported me and us on this journey along the way.

Personally, on top of running Gresham

The Little Book of Crypto

International - I speak, I write, and I have been featured in major publications across the globe including Forbes, CNBC, Bangkok Post and many others. The most surreal moment of my life was when I was flying on Easyjet to a conference I was speaking at in Monaco, while reading my interview in their inflight magazine. Small things.

I have consulted with governments all over the globe including those in the UK, Dubai, Labuan and other locations. There have been some amazing parts of my career and I am looking forward to the future and what that has in store.

Flashing forward to today I am fortunate enough to own and operate an international company which means I can afford a few nice things, not in any greedy sense, but indeed having come a long way from needing to repair

Chapter 1 - Intro

broken PC's at university to make money. All of that is thanks to the crypto industry. This success didn't come without hard work, but it also came from people helping me out. In the spirit of the crypto industry, that was what this was all about. I am as grateful to them for the opportunity as I hope they are to me having worked for and with them.

Crypto, in its truest sense, represents so many good things about people when they have the freedom to work together. We have the ability to use it as a good base line for how people will act if they are left to develop things in their own time. Of course, none of this is perfect, yet when we have seen crypto deployed in some situations it has lead to amazing ripples in the ocean of our society. I still see this spirit today at the shows I attend and in the founders of the projects and companies we work with.

One great example of this is in impoverished countries that are facing tough social and economic sanctions such as Zimbabwe and Venezuela. While these countries are facing issues that many before them have faced such as hyper inflation, unemployment, and stricter finance controls, Bitcoin and Crypto in general has allowed the citizens of these countries to actually improve their situation. In essence, Bitcoin removes isolation that comes from being a citizen in a country with a rough financial situation.

Although it is impossible for Bitcoin to solve the physical political situation, what it does allow is the freedom for many of the citizens of that country to trade with the outside world for, even on a basic level, some services. This exposure to the outside world is a

Chapter 1 - Intro

lifeline in a country that can't pay for goods and services. For the first time people who are poor and desperate do not have to turn to the most basic of human wants in order to pay for basic things such as food and water.

Additionally, there is the smaller side of issues which crypto can help with. During a study undertaken by my team, we ran a demonstration on how a coin placed into 'desperate or emergency situations' would have a massive impact. We simulated a refugee camp and the homeless population of a city. When the simulation was run in a conceptual part, the findings were amazing. A sad fact of many refugee camps is rape, abuse, and neglect. Many of these situations come about due to a lack of protection and a lack of people being able to survive. Most of the time this is because there is a lack of trading ability between people within the camp itself. So people are forced to use what they have or what they can acquire in order to survive, in a basic trade for trade sense. A sad fact of life, yet however, when a coin is introduced into the mix, which holds a currency value and something which can be traded into the outside world, the situation shifts dramatically.

Although many refugees may have some money, the big problem becomes: what is the best currency to use? Do you use the currency of the country from where those people have left? Or the currency of the place they are based at? Or perhaps an international one, such as the USD? Who is keeping track of what is worth? Where do you put it to keep it safe?
With individuals being able to use a crypto, earn it, spend it, and trade it, many of the individuals suffered much less of the consequences associated

Chapter 1 - Intro

with being in their position. For example, it was forecasted that prostitution would drop 67%, because people would not have to use their bodies to trade for things, but rather could earn money in other ways both in the camp and in the outside world. Of course, the currency could be received in donations, directly by the individuals and not by charities which would only distribute (in some cases) as little as 5% of every dollar made to the people on the ground.

The same improvement proved true for homeless people living in a major city. With restrictions placed on what they could and could not do with the funds, people were able to help and work themselves out of their situation. Although control of funds seems contrary to the whole premise of crypto, and still remains a controversial point, during simulations and questions it was concluded that many of the homeless would, sadly, use the funds for counteractive things which would not help their situation. After all, desperate times lead to desperate decisions being made. The concept was that homeless people should not be able to buy things they didn't need to survive; politics aside, when you are on a tight budget luxuries go out the window. The same is true for everyone regardless of their financial situation.

Now, many people in desperate situations do not want help or charity. They simply want the ability to be free, to be able to get themselves out of the situation they find themselves in. Crypto affords people the economic freedom to interact with the world on a international level. So when their current situation is dire, those in better situations are able to help. Many would argue, in the way they should be.

Chapter 1 - Intro

Without governments, without banks, without charities. Just giving people the opportunity to make money, spend it, and live in peace. At the end of the day, isn't that what we all want to do in life?

Crypto isn't perfect, and it really doesn't solve every problem. It has been aligned with the bag guys from time to time and that remains the stick that the big governments will continue to look at crypto through. However, for those of us that look beyond the bad guys and what the possibilities of crypto are, there is little to no doubt that in the future everything will be traded in digital currencies rather than what we have today.

In this book, I am going to walk you through where the market is today, and what the future might look like.

Chapter 2 - The law?

When it comes to Crypto, there could (and will be) a whole series of books written about its laws. The first thing that you should know, though, is that the world of crypto can best be described as the wild west of the legal world. In its truest sense.

Each country, each state and each city has its own laws. All of which often contradict each other. The laws are different in each region and each continent. Every country or jurisdictions leading authority may have a set of laws that is contradicted from one state to another under its control. Sounds confusing? Believe me, it is.

This lack of clarity is the reason why I started this chapter with a question mark, because 'the law' is such a fluid concept in this industry. We sometimes

Chapter 2 - The Law?

sit in the grey, firmly between the black and white. While 99% of people working in the industry simply want to stay legal, the complex framework and contradictory laws found within countries means that it is almost impossible to stay 100% legal even if you want to. Of course, that doesn't change looking at future laws. Sometimes even the experts you rely on won't know the answer you are really looking for.

We can see examples everywhere. Hong Kong, Taiwan, Macau and Mainland China all have different laws on crypto and on how people can own and use them. Despite all being the same country. The United States has different laws for each state as well as at a federal level. The European Union member states each have totally different laws on crypto and the European Central Bank has made up

The Little Book of Crypto

relatively few laws around it. It is enough to make your head spin.

The purpose of this book is not to educate you on the law. After all, if I taught you everything I knew about crypto there is a possibility I would be out of a job!

(Although I am seriously doubtful that that amount of knowledge could be put into one book).

Twinning that with the fact that the laws change on a daily basis, such a book would be almost useless by the time it went to print.

There are a number of reasons for the discrepancies and inconsistencies I mentioned above.

Crypto, unlike other technology sets, has massive financial and social

Chapter 2 - The Law?

implications through its growth. On many different levels. For the first time in possibly the history of mankind a new technology has outplayed the regulators in its growth. Where as many regulators didn't see Bitcoin as a major issue when it was first established, with its massive growth and price ever going up it has now become somewhat of an issue. However, as with everything, regulators coming late to the party means that they are having to catch up on a technology which already has a whole industry built around it. One which is paying taxes, employing people and fueling growth.

Because crypto is a brand new technology set, carrying with it many new other technologies, regulators will often at times struggle to understand what it is or what it means. We have seen this disconnect with regulators in the United States, not just with crypto.

The Little Book of Crypto

In congressional hearings on privacy laws with technology firms, the United States showed the world how many of the older generation struggle to understand even the most basic of technology concepts. Where there is a lack of understanding, there is a lack of tangible laws.

I worked with the government of Labuan when they were developing their regulators on Security Tokens (we will discuss these later in the book). What this region did was to look at industry experts and then develop laws based on what the industry needed: how they could best serve, how they could best deal with and develop a framework to encourage growth while keeping people protected.

The main job of the regulators is to protect people. However, in the instance of crypto, we have seen that

Chapter 2 - The Law?

line of protection ever encroach onto control. There is an old maxim that tell us that people should not be scared of their governments, rather that governments should be scared of their people. This stands as no anarchists' cookbook, however we have to point out the irony: for the first time, people are working together without their governments, and all the governments can do is try and keep up. The power of people working together is boundless.

People want to use Bitcoin and other crypto. We can tell that by the growth of the industry itself, the raise in price, and an overall explosion that has been ignored by many all along the way. Bitcoin and crypto have overcome every obstacle that has been put on their way. And there have been many obstacles.

In a social sense, Bitcoin allows the

freedom that people have always looked for. It actually takes many people back in time, in a transaction sense, not forward. Have you ever watched those old movies when someone throws a bag of coins at another person? They aren't too sure how many coins are in that bag, just that it's enough. Well, crypto is a little bit like that. People can set their own price to do whatever transactions they see fit with each other, this is why there is also no set denomination of crypto. Think about it in the basic sense, how do you break up a dollar? Into 100, 50, 20, 10, 5, 1, 0.5, 0.25, 0.05, 0.01. Have you ever asked yourself why? Why do we break down the dollar into that amount? Think of the impact this has on the market: if this is the set breakdown of things, it follows that this would have a direct impact on prices. Sellers will round things up to make it easier to pay for. So, the simple answer to this question

Chapter 2 - The Law?

is: because your government sets the demonization of your currency. This also includes how many decimals we break this down into. All currencies break down into two decimal places, never any lower than 0.10. Some go much higher, into the trillions, but none will ever go lower than this. When this denomination didn't exist (when people threw gold coins at each other) they could charge what they wanted and how much they wanted based on how many gold coins they wanted to receive.

Ok, I take your point, I am sure it wasn't quite THAT rudimentary. However, the point still stands.

All of this means one key thing. The laws for what is happening in the crypto space have already been written, as people have been trading freely for hundreds of years before the level of government control we are seeing today. At a time when governments struggled to get communication out to people, they still managed to buy and sell goods and services for money. The laws were made to protect people in those situations. What has happened is that over time, with the advancements of technology and the world becoming a smaller place, governments have obtained more and more control and so have much more say over what happens in an economical sense. This is not always a bad thing, but in a world where your bank can pay for your politicians election, and where big firms pay ex presidents wives $300,000 to speak at a conference, then we do have to wonder, have we reached the tipping point?

Truly International
Crypto is truly international. In every sense of the word. So, your local law

Chapter 2 - The Law?

firm or in-house counsel is not going to be able to help you. That's the first thing you need to learn. I play well with other lawyers, yet it can be often mind blowing the amount of times that local or in-house counsel does not understand what is happening.

If your local lawyer has never done anything internationally or is only qualified to practice in one jurisdiction, they probably aren't the lawyer for you. The problem with single practice lawyers is that they push the location or jurisdiction they know without knowing fully what the impact of crypto is. I can only tell of the amount of times people will ask me 'where is the best jurisdiction to host your crypto raise?' and expect a serious answer. To answer that question, you need to know so many things in advance. Of course, Estonian lawyers say Estonia, guys who have done their projects in Singapore say Singapore, and law firms with satellite offices in Malta, say Malta. You see the trend? Stick with a firm that has no loyalty to anywhere in particular. The term is agnostic. Their job is to serve you, not to serve a particular location.

Many countries have amazing incentives and options for companies that are looking to operate crypto, blockchain, mining, or undertake crypto raises. For this, research is everything. Also, currently there are so many differences in the field, that selecting the wrong jurisdiction could make or break your project. So take it seriously, especially if you're in startup mode. Spend your time doing your research and speak to professionals. Company location and relocation is a serious matter; just grabbing your local lawyer or using an online agent is not the best idea by a long shot. It's interesting that around 99% of our clients in America

Chapter 2 - The Law?

don't know about foreign control corporation laws. Think what else you don't know in your jurisdiction that could land you with fines, or even worse, jail.

The best projects will develop a legal team to work with them. The biggest and best conversations I ever have with potential clients is where they realize that they have a hole in their team and they are trying to plug it. This is to say that getting the skills needed is a massive step. Focus on that internationally. If you chose to participate in a crypto raise or work with a crypto company, you should always look at their team. Take a look at these questions: are they international, do they cover the globe, are there some massive gaps? Understand the laws surrounding crypto where you are based first before you go looking into other places, especially if you are taking part in a crypto raise or thinking of buying some crypto on the market. Check out your tax situation, your legal situation, how you can buy it and how you can sell it. Do not rely on any websites to give you information. If you have any questions, you should always find a lawyer that can help you. If you are looking for local information, this is the one time I would recommend using a local lawyer; that makes sense.

Because of the truly international sense of crypto you do have options. If you can't trade or sell crypto where you are, where could you? Can you set up a company there and do trading through that company? Start thinking globally and stop thinking locally.

Some governments accept it while others hate it
Within the international landscape of crypto, there is a huge amount of

Chapter 2 - The Law?

difference of opinion between governments and their agencies. This difference of opinion varies from agency to agency and governments to governments. There can be no over exaggeration when I say that crypto is the single most differential matter across the globe. No two countries really look at crypto in the same light, and certainly not every crypto in every class. For something which is being used by many members of the general public, it would have been assumed that there would be some kind of consensus achieved at least at a broad level. However, even the World Bank and the International Monetary Fund have done little to set any kind of stable position on what the laws around crypto should be.

The simple fact is that some governments denounce it. Some governments embrace it. Some tax it.

The Little Book of Crypto

Some denounce and tax it. The situation is enough to make your head spin. This is also compounded in countries that have complex internal political structure. For example, the United States has conflicting laws at Federal and State level, and the situation is made worse by some judges classifying crypto as commodity while others do not, and for instance, also some states requiring a license for any kind of activity. On top of that, there are the four financial bodies that claim to have jurisdiction over it. Oh, and the tax authority that wants its slice of the pie for any funds that are made. See, the situation in America is so complex, that even one of the biggest companies in the world, Facebook, decided that launching their coin within the country was more controversial than wearing a bright red hat with the words MAGA written on it in public. Congress was involved in their decision.

Chapter 2 - The Law?

On the other hand, some governments love crypto. Estonia is a great example of this. Estonia has taken the time to implement laws around the creation of Crypto specific licenses within the country that relate specifically to the trading and issuing of crypto. This means, under the current law, those companies that are looking to undertake a crypto raise (we will look at this later in the book) or companies that are looking to run an exchange (also looked at later) will have a license to do so; providing that they meet the criteria and maintain their compliance, the company can operate totally within the realm of the law. Now, flipping back to our earlier comment about banks, in case you were wondering: no, most of these companies cannot get bank accounts. Despite the fact that they are undertaking a totally legal issue with a license issued by the government. Insanity. We have seen this with other locations such as Malta which have also created similar licenses for companies that are operating from their country.

The European Union actually stands as a great example of where crypto has such a diverse existence. Malta and Estonia are working with companies to operate within the industry, including granting them licenses and welcoming their investment into the ecosystem. On the other hand, some countries within the EU do not recognize crypto at all. For example, Greece does not allow its citizens to buy or own Bitcoin or any other Cryptocurrency. Then, there are countries like the United Kingdom (ignoring Brexit) who have no position on cryptocurrency other than acknowledging its existence and cautioning people to be sensible when using it. Some years will have to pass before we have a standardized approach to crypto overall.

Chapter 2 - The Law?

Much of this difference of opinion comes from confusion. Many legislators are simply confused as to what crypto is and what it can do, reminding constantly the public of stories like Silk Road, a website which let people buy things on the dark web, a place that no human should ever need or have access to. Sadly, it seems hard to shake that bad view associated with the early days of Bitcoin and crypto in general.However, we all know how hard it can be to build a reputation. This situation was made much worse by crypto raises and companies selling crypto in order to raise cash. When some of these turned out to be actually fake, some people lost money. This was the point where the regulators really took notice. Regulators, as hard as they work, will often find it hard.

Private companies also set their own rules

The Little Book of Crypto

It goes without saying that where there are limited or no rules around a subject, others are free to make up their own. In the absence of information, something is better than nothing. So, many companies will establish their own rules around crypto and how it can and should be used within their realm; this includes brokers, exchanges or any other company which might be involved in the space.

Another great example we see of this are NGOs such as the British Blockchain Association. The BBA focus its work on blockchain and the crypto space, among other blockchain related areas, and produces a scientific journal that has been published in some of the largest academic databases in the world. Their work goes a long way to the main adaptation of crypto and blockchain but more so toward the proper governance of these two

Chapter 2 - The Law?

technology sets.

While it is appreciated that these companies and NGO's cannot be 'legislators' as we said before, in the absence of any clear guidance from the regulators or legislation bodies within various countries, these parties can help give some kind of guidance and uniformity to the industry while living through this period of time in where there is not too much solidarity happening.

Buying and Owning Crypto
Buying and owning crypto is the most important thing to understand before you even get into the crypto market. What are the laws around what you are doing, are you legally allowed to buy it, can you own it, what are the requirements if you sell it at a profit? All of those are important questions, and they are sadly onesI cannot answer for

you; what I can do here instead is give you a good list of what you need to be asking before you get involved in crypto. These questions include:

1. What is crypto classed as (including legacy and utility tokens)
2. How can you legally buy it
3. Can you legally sell it
4. What are your profits classed as
5. What reporting requirements do you have
6. Does your bank accept transactions from companies working in the space

Once you have the answers to these questions you should be in a much better position to understand how you can begin your crypto journey. You can find out all of these answers by getting in touch with a local lawyer. As you may remember, earlier in this book I spoke about lawyers in the crypto space when I introduced myself. I was being honest:

Chapter 2 - The Law?

if you need good information about crypto in your location then you should use a local qualified lawyer. Even if they don't have the answers they are still trained to be able to find them. However, for crypto on a much bigger sense, such as running an international crypto company, a more expert touch will be needed.

The most important thing above all else is that you remain safe in the eyes of the law. There is no point in breaking it just because you are looking to become involved in the crypto market, whatever your reason. Oh, and make sure that you keep your eyes on it constantly, as it will always change over time due to technology and market changes.

Running a Crypto Company
If you are working in the crypto space in a professional capacity, or thinking about it, the whole situation becomes

even more complicated. Before we even get into the deep stuff on this topic, let's pause and highlight the fact that if your website or company name so much as whispers the word "crypto', your company will not be able to gain any kind of bank account. This is because of the banks' blanket ban on cryptocurrency. We explored this earlier.

Entering the crypto market in a professional sense can be an incredibly profitable thing to do, providing that you meet the standards demanded by the industry. I am proud to have worked with many different clients in different sectors that now operate very successful international businesses only within the crypto space. This ranges from crypto mining, crypto media, crypto news, exchanges or others.

When you enter the crypto space in a professional capacity the first thing you

Chapter 2 - The Law?

absolutely have to do is complete due diligence, on everything. This is much more than simple market research like most company founders do. Due diligence involves everything from understanding how your business will conduct itself to where will it be conducted from. Because of the diverse categories of crypto all over the world, what you do in one location could be quite a simple business process, whereas in other parts of the world it could be a fully regulated activity by a regulatory body. Don't be fooled into thinking that just because you know the law in your own country you are safe everywhere. Knowing the law in your own country will protect you and your personal dealings. The minute you start working with individuals and companies outside of your jurisdiction, the minute you enter an international market.

This should not be seen as a bad thing,

after all, an international landscape gives rise to a multitude of opportunities. If you will be working with international clients in an international market, you should be opening your horizons. Opening a corporation in a location you may never have thought of before can have massive benefits, not only regulatory ones. Ensuring that your company is based at a good place is a solid starting block. After all, if you are going to work in such an international market, why close your doors to a section of that simply because you don't want to open an international corporation.

Consider what your company will be doing and then research which locations offer the most favorable location from where it would be possible to run that specific type of business. Please don't mistake the typical financial world with the crypto

Chapter 2 - The Law?

world. I have seen many companies open up in, for example, Hong Kong or Singapore because they believe it will give their business a better reputation. The truth of the matter is that these locations, while great for some things, are not the best place to open, say, a crypto mining firm. The whole selection process should be a marriage of laws, licenses, and ease of tax. After all, each one of these can differ from country to country as far as crypto is concerned. This decision matrix changes slightly if you are planning on doing a crypto raise. I will speak about that in a moment.

Finally, you need to consider how your company is going to operate in a financial sense. A number of companies we have worked with will not consider how they are going to be paid by their clients for their goods or services. An example of this is when a company working in the crypto space begins to work with people precisely in the crypto space; they may from time to time ask why a company also operating in the space does not take crypto as payment. The issue here is, if your whole company is set up to only take payment from fiat based currencies, this may sway away some of your potential clients or customers, simply for no other reason than the fact that it is hard for them to actually make a payment to you. On the flip side of this, if you do take crypto only as payment, how will you pay for things such as your office and electricity? I highly doubt that your landlord or your electric company will accept crypto as payment. So, in this instance you will need to make provisions to take funds from your clients, and then convert that into fiat based currency to pay your bills. When this happens you enter into the world of potential money laundering problems.

Chapter 2 - The Law?

Money Laundering
Money laundering is a massive consideration and concern within the crypto space. Crypto allows fast, effective, and mostly confidential transactions to take place. So naturally, in some circumstances, it has the ability to be used by individuals to launder money. Just as a reminder, money laundering is the process of taking funds that have been obtained during illegal activities and 'cleaning' them so that they can re-enter circulation.

Of course, as long as the usual anti-money laundering and Know Your Client rules are deployed through your business, you should keep yourself out of harm. Familiarize yourself with these on an international scale, not just the ones native to where your country is based. It's important to remember that when it comes to anti-money laundering it is not just your business that's impacted, it is society at large.

Ensuring that you collect information on all of your clients is the pillar stone of fighting money laundering, in a personal, corporate, and transactional sense. Being able to identify where funds came from and where they are going to, and by who was what done by is massively important. Retaining the data is the next step. In the event that the authorities need information on any transactions which have occurred, your responsibility is to pass them the necessary information over.

Of course, all of this will vary from state to state and country to country and totally depends upon what your company actually does. However, as you work in the crypto space, it is much smarter to play it safe than sorry, and of course it goes without saying that the closer you get to transferring or

Chapter 2 - The Law?

facilitating transactions (such as an exchange) the higher and tighter these standards are. As I spoke about a moment ago, if you are taking crypto and changing it into fiat, you need to ensure that the funds you receive are not being taken from a less than reputable source. Now, it is fair to also say that you cannot be responsible for where the funds have originated, yet if you are the reason the funds are converted back into fiat currency, then you become the re-entry point for illegal funds back into fiat. If you have a switch mechanism in your company for being paid in crypto, you should ensure that you collect client ID.

Operating a Crypto Raise
Crypto Raises is something we will look at later in this book in detail. Essentially, just as an overview, a crypto raise is the way in which companies will raise funds by issuing their own crypto and selling it

to members of the public. It is easily the most legally contentious area of the whole crypto sphere.

Essentially, there could be a whole book written on the laws of crypto raises. To be clear, countries can look at crypto and crypto raises in quite many different ways. Most countries are totally ok with Bitcoin (and other legacy coins) but have a major problem with any kind of crypto raise.

Regulators
The regulators are both the best friend and worst enemy of the crypto market. For the most part it is not bad decisions which have held the market back and caused confusion, it is instead the lack of any decisions which have fueled an indecisive market.
The lack of affirmative position by many regulators has allowed people to operate in a grey market. "Grey market"

Chapter 2 - The Law?

meaning that what they are doing is neither legal or illegal based upon certain aspects of their projects. The lack of indecision by many regulators in practice means that companies who simply want to be as legal as they possibly can, are being forced to take an unnecessary risk or to move to a jurisdiction where the law is clear.

Putting this into perspective, we know that the crypto raise industry is a multi billion dollar industry. This includes all the service providers, marketeers, market makers, experts, advisors and many other third parties. A large number of those companies would like to operate within the US, and this is a natural choice, since US is one of the largest markets on the planet and the home of a large amount of innovation. However, because of the sheer lack of regulatory oversight on the part of the regulators, the industry has been forced to move away and avoid the US altogether in most respects. Those who do operate in the industry within the US run the risk of being fined or put in jail for breaking security laws. And just to clarify, security laws which in this case may or may not apply to their activities. We saw recently TokenLot and ICO box both being fined by the SEC with prosecutions pending. These were both companies that were operating within the US. Now, it is granted that both of these companies were engaging in the sale of ICO tokens to US citizens and residents, which we know, now in hindsight, may have been a slightly bad move. However, without defending them, it is obvious that the law itself was not clear, and the Securities Act is being applied to something which may or may not be a security AFTER the fact. This means that even though those companies probably believed they were in compliance with the law, after looking

Chapter 2 - The Law?

at the Securities Act, assessing the market, and maybe even consulting counsel, the reality is that the SEC are changing the law to suit their needs.

The job of the regulators is to protect people and to uphold the law, not to make up the law as they go along. They are not part of the legislature. Having dealt with the SEC and others, I have seen sometimes that their team seems to forget that this is the case. Rather than working to check that no one was harmed by a company activity, and working with companies to apply the laws to ICO's (at the time), their view has been to just stamp down on some companies and use others as examples. In a market where the USA could benefit from billions of dollars of income, the SEC has seemed more interested in assuring that companies who sold something which may or may not have been a security (with a lack of clear guidance from their office) is now enforced with millions of dollars worth of fines and jail threats. Even though most of these companies pass the Howey Test.

We can flip that and compare it to two other locations, Estonia and The United Kingdom. Both took very different views on Crypto Raises and Crypto currency all together. Estonia implemented an ICO license, which allows companies looking to raise funds a license to be regulated to make money by the sale of utility tokens. They twinned this with other licenses such as a digital wallet (wallet to hold crypto) and exchange license. The introduction of these licenses meant that the companies looking to sell or trade crypto are regulated, have to pass police checks, and appoint responsible people to run the company. Sounds like a pretty fair situation, right? Now, this is no

Chapter 2 - The Law?

endorsement of Estonia, as there are many other locations that do crypto business, but this should be seen as a good example of how things can be regulated so that everyone can win. People can be protected, regulators can get information to conduct oversight, the national government can receive taxes to benefit the country. The tiny country of Estonia saw an influx of new companies looking to get in the crypto space.

We can compare now this to the United Kingdom, which has taken a relatively relaxed approach to the whole crypto scene. The regulators in the United Kingdom have taken the position of allowing the market to be free when it comes to crypto. Sure, those looking to work in the Security Token area have to comply with the laws, as is expected of any company working in the Security Token realm, but the market and laws are there for companies to work with (similar to all other locations). The flip side of that is that companies that are working in the utility token space are relatively free to do what they want in the current climate. The UK has strict anti-money laundering laws, and as long as companies comply with those, the sale, trade, issue, and dealing in utility tokens is regarded as a non regulated activity. The British Blockchain and Crypto Taskforce (of which I assisted) took one look at crypto and concluded that, realistically, the market was small, the options were limited, and people should be free to choose to enter into it. A comparison was drawn between those who want to purchase expensive wine and keep it, in the hope it may or may not go up in value. Freedom to own things in a speculative nature is considered a right in the UK. Not so much as those looking to buy stocks, shares, or

Chapter 2 - The Law?

commodities; those are regulated at the national level. However, the UK stands as an example of a location where companies can conduct work freely within the crypto space. Much like Estonia, we saw a massive influx of new crypto companies moving to the UK, taking advantage of the friendly nature of the industry. In light of Brexit, and the UK's departure from the EU, many have commented that Crypto represents a great opportunity for the UK to set itself up as a market leader.

A final note has to be written about multinational bodies such as the European Union. The EU sets monetary and financial policy for all of its member states. Actually, being a member of the EU requires that the member state will comply with the laws as set down by the European Central Bank and other financial regulators, in order to ensure harmony across the member states.

The Little Book of Crypto

The EU has taken a proactive stance on Crypto, balancing it between the protection of its citizens and the freedom of its member states to regulate them within their boarders. Notice was taken of Malta and Estonia benefitting massively from the new crypto craze. These member states were basically told that as long as companies comply with AML and KYC requirements (that aim at stopping the laundering of financial funds from terrorists or other criminals), the member states could do whatever they needed or wanted in respect of the space. Of course, the commission also thought of Switzerland when looking at the crypto space and included those member states which form part of the trading block as a whole, not just the EU member states.

The EU laws relating to securities apply to Security Tokens almost perfectly, and many companies now work within that

Chapter 2 - The Law?

space freely issuing and dealing in security tokens.

The most important thing to do with any Crypto project when considering where to establish yourself is to look at what the domestic and international laws are around your project. Look at possible future movements and if in doubt contact regulators to get their feelings on the subject!

Chapter 3 - Types of Crypto

As I mentioned earlier, there are many different types of Crypto. In this chapter, we are going to explore them. Understanding the different types of crypto will let you know where should you be participating and what you can or cannot buy, trade, or sell within your jurisdiction. It will also give you a much better understanding of the market overall and help you build your trading strategy. Please remember that this isn't a 'text book' guide of what these crypto's are or are not. We are going to talk about them in an honest way.

As with everything in crypto, nothing is straight forward. In this instance, we know there are different types of crypto; nevertheless,I should point out that there is no 'universal' method by which we classify them. Many people have tried, but my feeling has always been

Chapter 3 - Types of Crypto

that they have missed the mark on a number of occasions, usually because they are preparing something which is designed to suit their needs. We see this unnecessary naming in other industries too, when someone may class one thing as another in order to better suit their needs.

Although there are common used 'terms' to describe coins, there is no 'official reference'; this can cause some confusion in the industry. In such a diverse market it is likely that these classifications have had to change, in order to deal with the shifting landscape. Because of this, it is probable that even after this book has been released, crypto will continue to change and add new classifications. In any event, what is contained in this chapter will give you a solid reference point, at least to begin with.

The Little Book of Crypto

To best understand how crypto is classed, we have to begin with the fundamentals. There are two main types of categories for Crypto: coins and tokens.

'Coins' was the original name used to describe mostly all crypto. This started with Bitcoin, and many organizations that developed their own crypto also referred to it as a 'coin'. This made sense: everyone understood the term coin and it was easily identifiable as an industry standard.

During the 2017 period, though, when Initial Coin Offerings were at their bloom (we will discuss them later in this book), the Securities and Exchange Commission within the US began clamping down on those who were selling 'digital coins'. Outside of digital coins, the SEC were, in general, clamping down on anyone selling

Chapter 3 - Types of Crypto

crypto during an Initial Coin Offering (ICO), classing it as an unregistered securities event. Etherium conducted an ICO event, before the SEC took a serious interest in them, and really set the precedent for how these could go. At the time, the most notable element about Etherium was that it had never referred to itself as a token. Its makers use a totally new technology set which, although fundamentally identical to all other crypto's at its core, was different in its methods.

As ICO's grew, the SEC started to take notice and do what they always do. Fine people. The industry had to get smarter. So, to develop a work around (as so many lawyers do), the 'Token' was created. This Token was different from a Coin as it was 'Utility in nature'. From the development of the Token came the SAFT, and various other types of purchase agreements; this meant that companies were not 'technically' selling coins but rather offering a future sale for tokens open to members of the public. Needless to say this change in model lasted no longer than approximately two months before the SEC shut that method down.

As many companies were looking for easy ways to sell their crypto (following other initial raises) the 'Token' fell more and more into common use. The concept was that a token could hold some kind of utility use and no actual financial value attached to it, unlike a 'coin' which, by name, necessitates some kind of use. If we pause to think about it, for some cases, this actually makes sense. If your token is more of an actual token used as part of, as an example, reward scheme, then it has nothing to do with being a coin.

Although there was initially some

Chapter 3 - Types of Crypto

skepticism around if this 'utility' classification existed at all, that position has now been cleaned up. Since the evolution of the market over the last few years and the development of some international laws, we now know this to categorically be the case. The important distinction here is that technologically the crypto/token itself has nothing to do with its type of classification. The term 'utility' or other is only made different by the classification of its 'use case' by the issuer. That's it. So as we have seen in the market, many tokens will use an ERC20 Ethereum based chain (I will come onto this later), however one company will say its a Utility Token while another will say it's their Coin.

Because this always seems confusing, I often give the example of comparing Crypto classifications to cars. There are different types of cars and different makers. The classifications as to Coin

The Little Book of Crypto

or Token are like an SUV versus a Sedan type of car. The understanding of what kind of crypto they are is comparable to the makers such as Mercedes or Volvo. However, ultimately the classification of the type of car and what it does comes down to the company that has put it into the market, not to the market itself.

Now we know that coins and tokens are the usual classification for all different types of crypto. We can now begin to look at the different types of crypto there is within those categories. To best do this, I have broken down each different type of crypto you will find in the market.

Legacy Coin
Legacy coins are those which have been in the market the longest time and have the biggest trading volume. Great examples of these are Bitcoin, Litecoin,

Chapter 3 - Types of Crypto

Etherium, Ripple, and Tron. There might be others, but as with everything else in crypto there is no 'official' classification as to what makes a legacy coin.

The characteristics of a legacy coin are easily identifiable. They are often used by other currencies to 'benchmark' their price, as an example, you can find out the price of an alt coin (explained in a moment) by either USD or a legacy coin such a bitcoin. These prices will be placed on listing websites such as coin market cap or exchanges such as Binance.

The legacy status makes them a 'master' coin. This means that you can freely trade these coins with other tokens both on exchanges or privately (you can trade anything with anything, as a matter of fact, but we are speaking about exchanges here). It is for this reason why a number of exchanges will not accept cash from their users, but will accept legacy coins for them to begin trading on their platform. Likewise, users can only withdraw legacy coins from an exchange if they wish to make a withdrawal.

Additionally, legacy coins are those most used in a cryptographic raise. Many companies looking to raise capital will not accept cash but will rather accept legacy coins in the place of cash. As explained earlier, these carry much less regulatory risk than accepting cash during the raise.

Legacy coins are most commonly used in contracts for crypto. Although there are so many to choose from, the similar fact is that the trading volume and ease to convert to fiat currency (if required) is simply not in place for the smaller tokens.

Chapter 3 - Types of Crypto

The Utility Token
The utility token is a token which serves a purpose within a company or project. Unlike a legacy coin it has only a 'nominal' value attached to it: any price that it has issued to it is in place, so that an aggregate value for transaction purposes can be ascertained.

I often compare utility tokens to airline miles. Although they have no actual price or 'cash' value, they do have a 'nominal' value. For example, I am looking to use my airline miles, and I have 100 miles and need to book a flight that is $100. If the company lets me offset all of my miles against the cost of the flight, I can realistically work out that the price of these miles is $1 per mile. The same is true of utility tokens.

Much like airline miles, I also cannot use them anywhere else without permission of the company. For example I can use the airline miles for their primary use (to trade for flights, get upgrades, or extra perks). However, sometimes the airline might let me trade those miles for extra things such as a toaster or speedboat. Additionally, I can also collect and use those air miles with other companies within the group. So I can pick up British Airways miles using United Airlines flights. The same is true of utility tokens. Interestingly, one reason why many airlines have looked at tokenizing theirs is because of the ease of use of crypto over an air miles system that is currently used by many airlines today.

The Payment Coin
The Payment coin is as it sounds. A coin that is used to pay for goods or services. This is in the literal sense a Cryptocurrency. Bitcoin is the most famous payment coin, it is accepted by companies internationally and can be

Chapter 3 - Types of Crypto

used in some locations to pay for taxes, services, well, to pay for just about anything. However, there are many others out there.

A payment coin is often minted by a private company (or in the case of Bitcoin, an unknown group/person). The benefit of digital payment being from Crypto is that it is not subject to the usual government controls and offers true international freedom. It uses the trustless system explained above, which enables individuals to undertake transactions without the need of any kind of banking facility. That is a huge advantage, especially in parts of the world where less than 5% of the population have access to a bank account.

A payment coin adopts its value from simple maths. The trading volume worked along side the trading amount over a 24 hour period twinned with the number of coins in total. We look at the formula in more depth later in this book.

The Reward Token
The reward token is much like any other reward scheme. It is awarded to people for some kind of participation or exchange of information. Great example of these are airlines' reward tokens which are based on the blockchain. Although these are clearly very different from the Payment of Utility Token, they use the same underlying technology.

Reward tokens are used by companies looking to incentivize individuals to use their service. Using a reward token has advantages over a utility token as the issuing body can choose exactly where it is used and where it can be exchanged. It is usual that a reward token will not be listed on any third party exchanges.

Chapter 3 - Types of Crypto

The Engine Coin
Engine coins are usually the most advanced type of coin that can be issued by a company or group. The engine coin is used in advanced technology projects that need some kind of way to 'power' the users' interaction with the technology.

For example, a Virtual Reality company may issue an engine coin to allow people to use their software, download code, or make edits to an open source part of the software that is available for use. Think of these as 'pay to play/interaction' tokens. They let individuals work on a project, individuals are then rewarded for their work, or then allow others to purchase/use upgrades or BETA versions of the software made available by a company.

Engine coins usually have a 'core' use within the project, meaning that the

The Little Book of Crypto

whole purpose of the project is fueled by the coin they have created. This whole project will fall apart without the coin and the coin would fail without the project. They are the most important type of crypto you will see out there in the industry. This is because the trading volume of these coins will typically be much higher than other coins in different classes.

Shit Coins
Shit Coins are exactly as they are called. Shit. They have little to no use and were often issued by a company that was looking to raise funds once upon a time. The company which issued them has subsequently died or has large problems keeping going. However, the token lives on powered by those who still use it for whatever reason.

Alternatively, a shit coin is one which

Chapter 3 - Types of Crypto

has been issued by a company which has no real use at all. The company could still be going but it has become common place to call their coin a shit coin as it doesn't really do anything other than sit on the exchange. In some cases, it never even made it to an exchange. Many companies sold these during the boom and failed to deliver, on a promise to get them listed or tradable moving forward. This means that the whole company failed to meet its objectives.

Stable Coins
Stable coins are those which are linked to an underlying set class. However, unlike security tokens (which are explored below) they do not actually convey any of the ownership rights onto the coin holders. The coin itself actually uses an asset class to 'shore up' the value of the coin. For example, USDT will use the US dollar as its anchor,

meaning that these coins will always track the value of the USD.

The formula for working out the value of these coins is totally different, as they follow the path of the underlying asset. One USDT will always be worth one dollar, no matter how many times a day USDT is traded or what its other figures are. Stable coins are also totally different as they will have the underlying asset locked into position.

As an example, if there are 1 million stable coins which track the US Dollar, there should be 1 million dollars locked away in a secure facility. This means that there is always the collateral to facilitate a total buy out. Unlike other crypto, the underlying asset being in situation is what gives the confidence to the market with these types of crypto. In and economical sense, it is actually incredibly clever.

Chapter 3 - Types of Crypto

However, there are mixed feelings from the community around stable coins. Many love them, many hate them. This is because a stable coin takes on the form of the old 'fiat' currency system. Remember the gold standard? With this, all money in the world was based on the concept that the government had an equal amount of gold to service the debt of the currency as it was exchanged. Also, did you know that the notes and coins in your pockets are nothing more than promises passed from one person to another? If you look at many currencies over the world, it features the words 'I promise to pay the holder on demand the sum of..". Yep, that note you hold was an agreement between you and the government to have them pay the debt should the owner ever demand the gold under which it was backed. This was known as the standard. This, twinned with the value of gold, was how many governments benched their currencies against each other. So they could know the true value of, for example, the pound against the dollar.

Through time governments have come off the gold standard, though. With models such as quantitive easing, governments are now just printing more and more money as they need. The loan you have as a note in your pocket is literally not worth the paper it's printed on. Shocking. This model takes many back to these days of government lead backing of a currency. Some see it as an archaic, and anti-ideal model to the crypto movement. Many see it as the 2.0 model of crypto, and some even see it as the way a government would issue a crypto if they decided to create a digital currency.

Chapter 3 - Types of Crypto

The Security Token

Next up, we have to discuss the security token. The security token is a totally different type of crypto that is issued by companies. All of the tokens above are usually trying to avoid being classed as some kind of security either by being a payment, utility, or reward token which users are free to use at their own discretion.

Security tokens' sale (depending on where they are issued) does not constitute a security. Just as we saw the United States changing the game from Coins to Tokens with their (lack of) legislative guidance, Security tokens were born from the industry looking to legitimize the raise aspect of their project. The point was made that if during the raise period, the government was going to look at Crypto as a security, then companies should start treating it as such.

Security tokens have typically been avoided within the industry. The reason for this is that there is no solid secondary market for companies and individuals to sell their security tokens on. Additionally, many of these security tokens also have a vesting (holding) period, depending on where in the world they are sold from. This means that the owner will not be able to use the tokens for anything within a specific period of time. However, they do have the advantage over the other token types of being physically registered with a regulatory body somewhere in the world. If the tokens and coins described in the other section represent a total freedom of sale in a new age, security tokens represent just the recreation of the wheel, taking existing securities laws and dumping crypto within it.

Security coins make sense with projects that don't mind offering some kind of

Chapter 3 - Types of Crypto

equity or going through the necessary registration process in order to get this done. Yet, many ask the question 'is there any point in issuing a crypto tied to the security'. It is argued that if the seller is looking to raise funds down the security model, they should just follow current securities laws and raise funds through VC firms.

The crucial element of a security token is that it links something to the project. By this we mean that it gives the owner some kind of right that is associated with the security or underlying asset that is owned by the project.

It is amazing, no, it is actually mind numbing, the number of projects that have sold 'security tokens' but don't actually link the token with anything to make it a security. The idea in their head is that they have filed and so they are a security. Let me ask you this, if I take

100 menus from a restaurant, sell them internationally from the United States using the Reg S exemption, have I sold a security? The answer is no. I have just sold something internationally, regardless of whether the new owners will one day want to sell those menus for profit or trade them for menus from other restaurants.

In order to be a true security token, the token has to be linked with either an asset or equity. You should always check to see if a security token is registered with any kind of authority.

The equity token
The equity token offers individuals the opportunity to obtain equity within a company which has been tokenized. It's that simple. Rather than selling paper shares, which are issued by a company when they want to raise funds, these companies will actually turn their share

Chapter 3 - Types of Crypto

registry into a 'digital' version of itself and then issue the security tokens off the back of that.

The maths are incredibly simple. If you want to sell 100,000 shares then you sell 100,000 tokens. In a technological sense companies will often use a fungible token. A fungible token is different from other tokens in that each token has issued a number within the chain. Essentially, they are given a digital signature.

In turn, each one of these tokens represents a share in the company. So it is easy to work out what your rights, responsibilities, and the resale value is for these tokens. This puts the company back into the realm of usual company 'sales' in respect of raising funds. Many old school investors will be used to these, and it will make them more comfortable. They can easily understand what they are getting and what the security is tied to. These tokens can then be issued with any kind of rights that the company wants to give. Some projects give their tokens voting rights, divided rights, and all carry the usual protections established by the company law in the jurisdiction where the token has been issued.

In essence, this is the best of both worlds for companies looking to raise funds. It has the sex appeal of being a crypto but it also has the financial backing of typical company stuff, that many investors will understand. These types of tokens can easily be sold internationally by a company as there are already laws within almost every location to sell shares domestically and internationally.

The Asset Token
If the equity token offers individuals

Chapter 3 - Types of Crypto

equity within a company, the asset token offers individuals a right to a portion of an asset. This may sound like a crazy idea, however the concept of dividing assets to sell is nothing new. If you have ever heard of a 'time share', you will know what I mean. If you haven't heard of a time share, you are missing nothing.

Still, if you don't know what a time share is... The time share is the concept of a vacation home in say, Mexico, being sold to a group of different people. Each one of those people will purchase a 'part' of the home and as a result get two weeks a year to stay there without needing to pay anything more. The back end of this deal is that the property owner still owns the property but raises some cash by letting people have a right to that asset. That right is letting them stay in the property.

The Little Book of Crypto

The concept of an asset token works in the same way: an underlying asset is divided into numerous parts. Each one of those parts is turned into a token and then the tokens are sold to buyers who now own a part of the rights to that underlying asset. Now, I stress, they don't get to keep or claim that asset. That would just be a straight sale of part of it. By purchasing the asset tokens you are getting to own a part of the rights to the item. Not the item itself.

Tokenizing works very well if the underlying asset is expensive or rare. Real estate is always great to tokenize, so is expensive art, or for instance sports cars. In fact, you could almost tokenize anything which may have some significant value.

A great example of this was a project I saw with a classic aircraft. The company which owned it was

Chapter 3 - Types of Crypto

desperately trying to raise funds to restore this beautiful machine. For those of you who care, it was a B17 bomber. The company sold tokens attached to the underlying asset. Each token represented a percentage 'ownership' of the aircraft and 'owners' were allowed to take two flights a year (with a pilot) provided they had enough of the tokens. They also received the token and a certificate was issued by the company. This meant that you could own a piece of this aircraft, and then when the aircraft went up in value (once it was repaired) you could then sell the tokens, and all of the right along with it, in theory, for more money.

Again, the reason many companies do this is because the sale of tokens represents a much easier, and in the current market, sexier sale than selling flat equity or rights in something. They are also much easier to trade, since proving your ownership in the asset or equity is easy. You have the tokens, unlike a database which the company would have to keep itself, which costs time, money, and effort, every time it needs to be updated when there is a sale.

Let's consider the alternative. If that aircraft owner wanted to use a typical model they would have to sell 'imaginary' equity, issue paper certificates, and then keep a record of who owns them. Every time the ownership would change, the owner would need to keep a record, update it and issue a new certificate. You would have to contact them and so would the new owner. We know from real life how hard it is to get people to give accurate information correctly, quickly. With the digitization of this process, the person who owns the tokens has the rights associated with them. That's it. True,

Chapter 3 - Types of Crypto

the same could be said of paper shares, however in this case you need to wonder: what stops fraud, or theft, or anyone keeping any kind of record of who or where those shares are if no central database is adopted. It doesn't.

The truth is when security tokens first became a thing I hated them. I still have very mixed emotions about them in the industry we are in today. Although there are obvious advantages for a project to issue a security token in some cases, I do feel that security tokens don't represent 'crypto' and what it is or stands for. The concept of crypto is that it is designed to be 'decentralized', not run by one person or organization. The minute a central regulatory body has control over the company that has issued the security token, the whole system goes out the window.

There are already so many different

ways for companies and individuals to register with a regulatory body and then raise cash that way. Many Venture Capital firms actually prefer that method as it is much easier for them to understand. So, the question has to be, what is the need for the company to issue a security token, and is it a real security? We will cover that more extensively when we look at taking part in an initial crypto sale that is done by a company.

Of course, I consider this with also the fact that there is actually no licensed secondary exchange for security tokens. So, even if you do buy them, you could be buying something which you can never sell on an open market such as other types of tokens. Although this may change in the future and there are now some new locations which are allowing the sale of security tokens to licensed companies, we are some way

Chapter 3 - Types of Crypto

off that market being as big as the other types of Crypto.

Identifying what a token does
What a token does within a project or company is massively important. The value of a particular crypto is tied to its 'use case,' which effectively means how much will the Crypto be used. Those crypto which are used more on a daily basis will be worth more money.

Because of this, when assessing a crypto and looking at what it does you need to fully understand how and what the token will be used for. Remember, if the answer is 'nothing' then it is a shitcoin. And we know we should avoid these. If it gives you equity and is registered, it's a security token, which could cause secondary trading issues and hold a vesting period. Finally, if it is given as a reward, it's a reward coin. You should take careful note as to what particular crypto does what, as the ones which have little to no use will not be worth much, and buying security tokens with vesting period will not help your strategy if you are looking to play short.

You can always find out what a token does by looking at the company's white paper and game plan. You should be able to answer the questions: what are its objectives 6, 12, and 24 months after the company has sold the token? What will the token's role be within the project, how will they be doing it? Also, are you able to trade it for other tokens or earn it by doing things with the company? You need to understand all of that in order to know if you are effectively looking at getting something which could end up as a shit coin, or if it actually has an ongoing use that can be used by people moving forward. This also means a REAL use, not just one which has been made up by the

Chapter 3 - Types of Crypto

company in order to make it seem like the crypto has a real use within a project. You can tell a real use from a fake use because it will make sense, it won't just be put into the project as some after thought.

Let's go back to the car analogy. A steering wheel is a key component of a car; you have to be able to turn it while you are driving. A spoiler (the thing on the back) is usually unnecessary (outside of a hyper or sports car). It is there for nothing more than show, and it is designed to make it look pretty and convince you to buy it. The same is with crypto. Does the token or coin have an actual use within the project, or is it nothing more than a shiny add to convince you to take part in it?

You should always be prepared to speak to the company issuing the token. We cover off some of the key things you should look at during the initial sale period during a crypto raise later in this book.

We will explore exchanges in more detail in this book, looking at what exchange does what. However, you should always do your research based on what you are looking for. That research should be based around what the token does and what type of token it is.

Futures Trading
As the market has evolved, we cannot leave off the new 'futures trading' model that has evolved around Bitcoin. Futures trading is where you can speculate on the price of an asset without actually owning the underlying asset itself. A great example of this is oil. If you wanted to be speculative (invest) on the price of oil because you think it is going to go up, the last thing

Chapter 3 - Types of Crypto

you want to do is actually go out and buy barrels of oil. Or perhaps you do, I don't know your personal situation and I don't judge. However, let's pretend that you're like the rest of us and don't want barrels of oil at your house. So rather than owning the oil, you purchase a 'futures contract' on the asset itself. This in effect means that you have purchased oil at a certain price, and you can lock in that price in the hope that someone will buy it from you in the future.

Options Trading
Options is a little similar to (pure) futures trading. However, it is not like futures trading. In here, if the price goes up, someone will hopefully buy the options contract form you, or you could simply let the options contract lapse if it is not worth as much as you had hoped.

This is one of the key reasons why we

know that Bitcoin (and in time, other crypto) will become more and more advanced. Many have begun to look at Bitcoin as a type of 'digital gold', where companies are now placing commodities (futures and options) trading on the asset itself without ever actually owing the asset. This could be something that you could do if you were used to a more ''typical' financial situation. However, be warned, it is not legal in every country and, more importantly, there is no insider trading laws around the crypto market.

So, while I am not naming any names, you should always keep in mind that the big broker you use will sell you an options contract from their commodities desk from the third floor, while in the meantime the crypto desk on the fifth floor is buying up all the bitcoin it can get its hands on in order to pump and dump the price with some of the other

Chapter 3 - Types of Crypto

bigger players. If anyone doubts this is happening, the community has already identified the wallet addresses of some of the major banks and financial institutions. Remember, I said earlier in this book that crypto is much more transparent than the traditional financial instruments you will be used to, that has both good and bad elements about it.

Chapter 4 - The Cryptographic Sale

The Cryptographic sale is one of the most important elements of the Crypto universe. In this chapter, I am going to walk you through what the different types of crypto raises are, what do they do, and the things you should look for before you participate. Crypto raises are one of the biggest areas I have worked in, so this chapter might be a little more in depth than the others, this is also the most complex topic (outside of law), so it may take you a few re-readings of the chapter to understand it fully.

Before we get in depth, it is a good idea to start with an overview of what the crypto raise is. I know the aim of this book is not to walk you through things in a 101 sense, but in this case there is

Chapter 4 - The Cryptographic Sale

so much information in the market around what the different types of raises are, that we need to go back to the basics in order to fully help you and other people understand it.

As you have seen in this book, there are different types of crypto. To go with that, there are different types of raises. Different crypto can be sold in different ways to different people. The law is so complex in this area that it is almost impossible to give a 110% accurate account of the whole landscape, a landscape which, by the way, is always shifting. If Crypto was the ocean, then the crypto raise would be the rip tide. Always moving and very deadly.

The concept of selling during a crypto raise is known as the primary market. It is the first time something is sold to a group of people, the same as the typical financial world. Once the crypto hits an exchange it is known as the secondary market. This is the period during which parties can trade the crypto with each other and swap it for other cryptos. It's important you know this, as these are very different phases in the crypto lifecycle, covered by different laws, problems, and parties.

The Initial Coin Offering
The Initial Coin Offering (ICO) is the original way in which companies would raise funds. During the 2017 period these were huge, with some participants making up to 200% returns on any coins they purchased early on in the offering.

The ICO is based around the concept that a company will sell its coins cheaper than they will be worth on the secondary market. The earlier you get involved with the sale, the cheaper you will be able to buy the tokens.

Chapter 4 - The Cryptographic Sale

Selling the coins usually begins with a 'white list' period. This is where the company will let individuals know they are planning on conducting an ICO and ask interested people to register on the company's website. The 'white list' is then split into two different categories. The alpha white list and the beta white list. The alpha white list is basically a fancy way of saying 'email list'. You are showing the company that you are interested in buying some of the tokens when they go on sale, and it also lets the company know how many people are interested in the sale itself. The beta white list is more advanced. It is a basic agreement between you and the company to purchase tokens when they go on sale, although it is not the full terms of the agreement and acts more like an MOU between you and the company. On the flip side, it lets the company know how many people are committed to buying the tokens when they come for sale. The beta white list will make its members undertake KYC (Know Your Client) checks, as well as have them fill out all of the information such as how much they want to spend, or how many tokens they want to purchase. The transaction is basically undertaken; everything except the physical transfer of funds which will be done when the tokens go on sale. We consider this almost like an early commitment.

After the white list phase the company enters into a 'pre-sale' phase. The pre-sale phase is where the coins are sold at the cheapest price. Only a certain amount will be available during this time for sale. It is this limited amount of tokens for sale which usually builds up the excitement, and twinning this with the number of users who have signed up on the white list, a company doing a solid ICO should sell out of these coins.

Chapter 4 - The Cryptographic Sale

Then there is the general sale phase. This is where the discount is applied through the sale time, so that individuals can buy the token at a discounted price. As time goes on, the price of the token will rise during the general sale period. The idea here is that the earlier someone takes part, the cheaper they will be able to buy tokens for, offering an incentive to get in sooner rather than later. This 'get in early, get it cheaper' principle is applied to almost every raise type. Rewarding those who choose to participate earlier.

Many say that the Initial Coin Offering slowly died toward the end of 2017. This was because the market took a massive crash, and projects were no longer raising millions of funds during an ICO. The reality of that situation is, in fact, that the market grew up and shifted, like a child that had finally hit its teenage years. During the 'hay day' companies could raise millions during an ICO which ran for a few weeks; this was huge. Companies such as Kodak and Telegram raised millions during a very short period of time. As 2017 ended, companies were struggling to raise even a million dollars. The market took a massive dive in general and a lot of crypto confidence died with it. While those of us saw the bubble coming to and end, those who were not used to the typical financial world were shocked when it finally changed. Nothing lasts forever.

Token Generation Event
At one point the ICO was also known by the name Token Generation Event. Remembering that the actual use of the crypto is defined by the company itself who is issuing the crypto, for those who were calling their issued crypto a 'token', it seemed counterintuitive to

Chapter 4 - The Cryptographic Sale

refer to the sale period as an ICO. Therefore, the term Token Generation Event was born. Part of the reason for this was also to find a workable model to get around securities bodies which had classed a digital 'coin' as a security, or the initial sale of a financial coin as a security event which needed to be registered. A TGE gave companies the ability to say 'we never undertook an ICO or sold a coin that was anything like financial in nature". However, as the market has grown, many have known that the TGE and the ICO are essentially the same thing.

The Initial Exchange Offering
The Initial Exchange Offering (IEO) is different from the Initial Coin Offering as the whole process of sale is conducted through an exchange. In the event of an IEO the company will sell its tokens through an exchange, which will manage the whole event. The exchange

is an already established company which will be using its trading platform to allow its users to take part in the initial sale. This rules out having to hunt down parties that are looking to purchase the tokens from you; the market already exists.

The advantage of conducting an IEO over an ICO is that the exchange is promoting it to its members that are already using the exchange. The hope is that those members will be enticed by the exchange offering something for the first time.

This is, however, the 2.0 model of the IEO. In the past, there was another way of conducting an IEO which has now become known as the 'airdrop'. This was when a company would give their tokens away for free on Exchanges to its members. The method was different from an ICO because people did not

Chapter 4 - The Cryptographic Sale

pay for the tokens; they were simply given them. This meant that they were free when they were first given away and then would increase in value as many people used them. Tron was a great example of how this can be done in practice. When the token was first launched, many people received it for free. However, the risk with the 1.0 model of an IEO was far too great: a company would have to produce billions of tokens to give them all away to millions of people. The problem with providing that many tokens comes from an economics point of view. Because of the sheer number of tokens it would be impossible for the token to break into the high value area. Meaning, the token will only ever be worth a few fraction of a cent.

The 2.0 model, however, comes with its own risks. I have never been a fan of the IEO unless it is conducted on a major exchange with a verifiable user base. Selling the token through an Exchange seems to be a local move, a ready client base who you can pitch and sell the token to is after all a dream for many companies. Yet, there are many pitfalls. As you can imagine, from a regulatory point of view, any company that wants to sell your token on your behalf and take a fee for doing so cannot argue that they are not, in some way, a type of broker. Where as under an ICO you can say you simply sold something to people, under an IEO you cannot get away from the fact that the sale is being done with the intention of speculation, 'the hope of making more money'. Many exchanges are not stupid to this fact and so have based themselves in locations which makes it hard for regulators to find the company owner. While I don't believe this is a problem in itself, that also means it's hard for those who wish to keep the

Chapter 4 - The Cryptographic Sale

company to its word to also find the company owners. It's for this exact reason why we have seen many 'scam' IEO's run. Not by companies producing fake tokens, but by exchanges lying about how much they have raised, how many people use their platform, and how much people can make.

As I conducted more research on this, it seems that rather than being the exception, such business practices are the norm for many exchanges. Manipulating numbers, fabricating trading volumes and raise amounts are standard business practice. In a perfect world an IEO would be a great way to raise some serious cash, yet many parties are being lied to about how successful this model really is. Therefore, before you even think about getting involved in an IEO you need to look more at the exchange itself than the company. Make sure the figures they are quoting are verified. You can do this by taking some common sense approaches: contact companies that have listed on their exchange, speak with their teams or their desk and ask for an honest assessment. If you are more advanced in the market, look at the trading volumes and see if you can spot 'bots' trading the Crypto. Bots making usual trades is an obvious sign that the trading volume on the exchange is mostly made up, and an IEO will not do well as there are limited 'real' users.

Both the ICO and the IEO are great ways of selling utility tokens into the market. They are not a good way of selling Security Tokens.

The Security Token Offering
The Security Token Offering (STO) is a very different model altogether. A security token is literally one which is

Chapter 4 - The Cryptographic Sale

registered with an authority somewhere in the world. You should refresh your memory with how it was explained earlier in this book if you need. This means that the sale is conducted in line with two sets of laws. Firstly, the raise will have to comply with the sale laws of where the security itself is registered and regulated. Secondly, each country will have its own laws around the sale of securities to its citizens and residents. This makes the STO much more complicated than the ICO/IEO offerings because they carry many more laws around them. They are also not open to everyone. The most common types of STO sale that we see encourage sales to 'qualified' or 'high net worth' investors. This is because those who have more money are usually allowed to spend it how they like. Ironic, considering that earlier in this book we spoke about banks stopping people from spending their money on crypto. If you ever needed an example of where the rich can do what they want and everyone else can't, here is one in practice.

Security tokens are usually sold under some kind of exemption or full registration. Each security offering will need to be registered in one location or more to enable it to have the rights to be sold. As you can imagine, this is a much more expensive proposition to those who are looking to raise funds for a company. The registrations, documents, and compliance are all more expensive. Twinning this with the fact that in most locations the tokens have to be sold by a licensed broker, many may wonder why do an STO at all. The simple answer is that it attracts more of the 'whales', those with more money, including VC firms.

The issue with utility token from a

Chapter 4 - The Cryptographic Sale

purchasers' point of view is that it has no 'tangibility', it gives no rights to those who own it other than the fact that they simply own a token. While this is ok for 'ordinary' people who are happy to understand the risk associated with utility tokens and their sale, those 'professional' people who are already working and playing in the financial world struggle to understand how a utility token works. While they love the concept of risk versus reward, they don't seem to like it if the value on both ends of the proposition is too high. This is especially true for those who are representing a financial investment firm, such as a VC or a family office. Justifying the investment is incredibly important to these financial bodies. Many other investments open to them offer equity, rights, and returns. If a manager was to report to its members that it had spent a large chunk of its funds on a non-regulated, non-secured proposition the members may start showing up at their house!

Likewise, with the tradeoff on regulation and being regulated for an offering, against being non regulated and closing its target market, the company undertaking the offering also receives more security. If ICO's are the true wild west of crypto and raising with them poses a logistical legal nightmare (as discussed earlier) the STO clears up a huge amount of that confusion and uncertainty. Essentially the company is making itself safer as far as regulation is concerned.

The STO valuation
Valuing an STO is a totally different situation altogether. Those who are used to the typical financial world will often look at a valuation of a company and work out how much it is worth based on a number of elements. These

Chapter 4 - The Cryptographic Sale

elements include forecast, income, performance, market sector, etc. All of these elements are combined to work out how much it is worth. The same is true of an asset. You know how much a painting is worth based on demand, rarity, etc. So would it make sense that an STO is based on the same valuation? No. An STO is valued totally differently than any other kind of financial raise. This is because unlike a traditional financial raise, there are a number of other factors at play.

The token itself is a different type of commodity to a share or a stock than what a typical company is issuing. As we saw with utility tokens, there is a trading volume which allows the value to be worked out. A security token is the same. If we compare a share in, say, Apple, Inc. which is valued based on how the company is performing and how the demand is for the share itself.

This is then twinned with company performance, etc. The initial sale is then evaluated based on the company forecast. With a Security token it works slightly different. To a large extent the value of the token is based totally on the demand of the token itself twinned with how many tokens are held by the company (think of this as issued capital versus reserve capital). The security token does not care how the company performs as it is unusual that a dividend will be issued on a security token, so the whole value is based around demand.

Of course, the whole situation is compounded by the lack of legal secondary market exchanges. Although there is talk of some opening up, but the reality is because of the complex nature of the Security Token industry, this means it will be some time before a feasible and well used exchange is

Chapter 4 - The Cryptographic Sale

open, meaning security tokens can be used on the secondary market.

The Hybrid Token Offering
The Hybrid Token offering is a unique solution which was developed some time ago. The logic is that a utility token offering (ICO) and a Security Token Offering (STO) are both legal just in different locations in the world. If you cast back to the law section you can refresh your memory around the countries which like utility tokens and those which prefer security tokens.

So, in order to raise funds and maximize a raise, companies will issue both a utility and a security token and conduct an ICO and an STO at different phases. The concept being that the security token will be sold in countries which accept it, and the utility token will likewise be issued in countries that accept it. Therefore, the company raising funds does not fall fowl of the law anywhere globally, and is able to solicit funds in some way or form in different locations internationally. This is a massive step for companies that are looking to stay legal and offer a little something for everyone.

This method has grown in popularity over the last few months (at the time of writing) because it is an astute step to attract all types of funds. With an HTO companies can offer something for almost everyone, from VC firms that can only justify security tokens with equity attached, and also for those who only want utility tokens.

The Pre-Sale period is the ICO, the sale of utility tokens. The Full-Sale is the STO or the sale of security tokens. This replaces the typical pre- and full sale periods with different tokens being offered at different times.

Chapter 4 - The Cryptographic Sale

The Initial Securities Offering
The Initial Securities offering is essentially an IEO using security tokens, which are sold through a licensed broker. The process is exactly the same as an IEO; however, the company undertaking the sale is a licensed financial entity that can sell securities.

This is a new concept which has not yet been explored or established. However, the market is most likely organically moving in that direction. At the moment, this is a pure speculative option, though. We will focus more on these later in this book.

Airdrop
The Airdrop is where crypto is given to a particular class of people either during the raise period or after it has concluded. An airdrop on a massive scale to all users of an exchange was the original 1.0 model of an IEO (see the

IEO section).

Now the Airdrop model is used to encourage people to have, hold, and use the token. For example, some companies may airdrop tokens to everyone that is in the company Telegram group after an ICO has finished. Or, a company may airdrop crypto to everyone that is attending a conference during a crypto raise.

The benefit of undertaking an airdrop is that it encourages people to use the crypto. Remember, the more that people use the particular coin or token, the more the value goes up. Airdrops can only be done for utility tokens.

Bounties
Bounties are received by individuals for doing something to assist the project during their raise phase. Such as sharing information over social media,

Chapter 4 - The Cryptographic Sale

encouraging new members, or participating within the Telegram Chat Group of the raise. Bounties are designed to encourage interaction within the community of a particular project, and help the project raise awareness of the project itself and the raise.

Bounties are similar to rewards, but a bounty usually suggests that something has to be done to earn it, whereas a reward is just given. Therefore, I won't explain reward tokens as I believe you can understand when people would receive a reward for doing something. Bounties are only available for utility tokens, the same as other raise ideas.

Bonuses
Bonuses are tokens which are issued to parties that enter the raise during a certain time. So, for example, those who purchase tokens before the end of

the first week of the sale, will receive a bonus of 200 tokens. Again, this is only open for utility tokens.

Rating Websites
Rating websites are, on the surface, a great idea. A website which ranks a crypto raise based on a number of key criteria. They assign the raise a rating based on how many of these criteria they pass or fail. Based on the score, individuals can then know the credibility of the project, confirm it's not a scam, and understand how reputable the experts working on the project are. In such a new and diverse market, getting more information is always a healthy thing.

At least, that was always the idea.

Many rating websites started out as a good idea, giving information to members of the general public who

Chapter 4 - The Cryptographic Sale

were looking at participating in ICO's. A trusted source of information in an otherwise unregulated environment. However, as with a number of unregulated activities, things went south very fast.

The 'Rating" companies quickly worked out that they could charge a premium service for companies that wanted to get their rating quicker. Of course, when money begun changing hands, the actual criteria for rating went out of the window, running off quicker than a guy who had just robbed a bank.

In true turncoat style, the ratings websites became as crooked as the ratings agencies servicing the 'typical' financial world. Yes, I'm looking at you 'ratings agencies'. The ICO ratings companies began using a 'pay to play' principal. As long as your money cleared into their account, you got a good rating.

The situation became worse when some of the larger ratings websites implemented an 'expert' scheme. These 'experts' could then score and rank projects that they were part of, improving the score of the actual project on the platform. This encouraged these experts to be appointed to projects, so that they could get a good score on the ratings websites.

Naturally, it goes without saying, many of these 'experts' did nothing to warrant the title of 'expert' other than just simply being on the rating site. This lead to all of these experts demanding, sometimes, thousands of dollars to join a project, even though they had never been in the finance, raise, or technology world in their lives. To make the situation better, these experts

Chapter 4 - The Cryptographic Sale

themselves worked out that they could sell their services personally. So experts had freelance sales people working on their behalf taking a percentage of the fees that the expert would charge. This meant that one company could receive proposals from a number of experts on the rating site, the rating site itself, and then other experts competing on their behalf.

All of this is documented in conversations and across news articles.

Obviously, because of this, so many rating websites are now utterly useless, including the largest in the industry. They created a monster and some of the public faces 'number 1 on xxx' became a serious problem in the industry. Many of these experts exploited projects by looking to simply raise credibility and stay transparent. Some of these individuals held themselves out as experts with absolutely no industry, financial, or useful knowledge. These companies still exist today, but they don't actually do or mean anything. They are as impacting as chewing gum on the sidewalk: annoying in every sense. Avoid ratings websites and do not believe what they say about any kind of project. The experts listed on their sites are often not experts.

Experts

This comes onto a much bigger point. First, assume that everyone who claims to be an expert in the field is talking absolute crap. This includes those who have an alignment to the profession and those who work for the big four. The truth is that we are all still learning this industry and there is no way it is old enough for anyone to be classed as an 'expert'. Even me, with my experience, would never call myself an 'expert'. In

Chapter 4 - The Cryptographic Sale

an industry so diverse, and so fast moving as this, it is almost impossible for someone to know everything about it!

The truth is that people are trying to make a quick 'buck' in the crypto industry. They are trying to develop hero status without actually saving the day. They will list themselves as experts, sales professionals, and investors, without having done anything before. Sure, they may have helped launch a few shit coins, but they won't have done anything with any real tangibility. So, you have to go old school when you approach and look at an expert, this includes when you are looking for investment, participation, or raise support. Wherever you sit in the spectrum, make calls, check them out, and do your due diligence, assume that everything they say and everything they have done is absolute shit. Guilty until proven innocent.

More importantly, this includes self publication and big names. Just because someone is a 'big name' in the industry don't be so desperate to believe everything they say. I have seen so many of these 'experts' show up, talk crap, and go home. There is an expression from the place where I am from: 'you've got nothing to say and you are saying it too loudly'; well, the crypto industry is the absolute existence of that. I could write a whole book on people that speak bullshit in this industry, people who do absolutely nothing, and people who have made a name for themselves out of talking nothing but absolute shit. That may be the next book, calling out the people who speak bullshit and the outrageous claims they have made. Watch this space. The golden rule is don't be taken back by what you see. Especially where

Chapter 4 - The Cryptographic Sale

self publication is provided. I could open an Youtube account, Twitter account, and drop a few million followers, throw up a video once a week, call it a show, invest $50k in nothing and then say I'm an investor. To give you an example, here are some true stories below. The names have been removed to protect the guilty.

A 'Finance Expert' that bought bitcoin some time ago through a government agency, using mostly the money acquired through his dad's hard work. They got lucky when the price went up and now they sit on stages and talk nothing but typical finance BS in a world that is actually so far from the financial world it's painful. So much so that they have simply stopped showing up to conferences to talk. They throw out a random prediction on how the price of Bitcoin will rise, forgetting that the rest of the world knows they have a

The Little Book of Crypto

50% chance of being right. Heads or tails.

A professional that created a show online to talk about ICO's. Again, talks mostly crap about projects they can't understand and tries to get projects to pay to be on their show. Hoping the views they rack up on Youtube will make them famous.

A Doctor who has social media showing them on private jets, attending conferences, and speaking about cryptocurrency. Forgets that after he spends the night drinking other people's vodka and then sits in the cab begging people he doesn't know to invest '50k' into a London based blockchain center, it won't be forgotten. I am yet to meet a guy who travels by private jet but has to go to strangers and beg for 50k. Side note, preliminary research shows the doctorate is fake as hell.

Chapter 4 - The Cryptographic Sale

Family office manager with no money. Fake deals. Access to over a billion dollars in assets, all of which turns out to be fake. Gets kicked from every major site.

These are just some examples of the kind of people that are held out as 'experts' in the crypto space, despite the fact that what comes out of their mouth is mostly absolute bullshit and their behavior is stupid. I have a sore spot for this. Just like lawyers who claim to be 'blockchain and crypto' experts but have no fucking idea what a hash rate is or how international nodes can properly be deployed.

The White Paper
The White Paper is the single most important document in a crypto raise. It is designed to give accurate and concise information around the project and its ambitions. It is not a 100% route

map and plan; it is however an overview of what the project is trying to achieve. For those of us who have written typical White Papers in the past, we appreciate that what is produced in the crypto industry is not, in fact, a white paper. A white paper in a typical sense is an expiatory document outlining the 10,000ft view of a project or idea that someone has had. A Crypto White paper has become more like an investment or prospectus document. Even though it is 100% not such a thing (enter disclaimer here). Wink wink.

You should always take the White Paper with a pinch, no, wait, a bucket of salt. It is made by people who may or may not have an idea what they are talking about, and it is almost always written by the cheapest source open to the project. It does give a good level of information around the project and should include key things such as token

Chapter 4 - The Cryptographic Sale

distribution, key dates, and the project information itself. When I have been involved in drafting white papers I have always said that they need to conform to something simple: Who, What, and Why?

If the talent or section in the document does not explain who, what, or why, then it should not be in there. A huge amount of white papers are not giving any accurate information around the project or what it does. However, you should absolutely read and understand it in order to understand the project fully. Also make sure that you thoroughly read the website of the project. Together they should compliment each other as to what the company is trying to do.

Remember to focus on two main things.
1. What is the company trying to do?
2. What will the token do?

The Little Book of Crypto

Just because the company has a really good idea this does not mean that their crypto will be a good thing. Sometimes, it is ok to admit that crypto might not be the best path for a project. Sometimes companies should look at going down the 'typical' financial route. There is a common misconception with Crypto raises, and this that it is usually believed that a crypto raise will lead to success. As a matter of fact, though, it was concluded that the amount of startups that make it past one year is around 20%. I believe that number halves for a company lasting three years down to 10%. That's in Silicone Valley alone.
Just because a company made money, had a great idea, and was successful in their raise does not mean their coin will not become a shit coin.
Ask yourself why the company is doing a raise. Is it because they have a crap idea that no VC firm will touch? Or, is it

Chapter 4 - The Cryptographic Sale

a great idea and the Crypto plays a key element in it? Balance the decision making between 'this is a great idea' and 'this crypto will do great'. The company itself has to survive after the crypto raise, so does the team have the ability to run a company if they do make millions of dollars?.

Why do a crypto raise
For the first time ordinary people can raise money for a great idea and not lose their control to the existence of the VC firms. People can raise money, keep their company, and help other people make money on the way. It's capitalism in its purest form.

Of course VC firms don't like the crypto raise. Imagine if people could make millions without losing equity (STO's aside). If you have ever worked with a VC firm then you know how much of a pound of flesh they will want to take in

The Little Book of Crypto

exchange for the money they are offering. It's also usually terrible terms for the company. Don't believe me? Ask the co founder of Facebook how he was fucked, the founding team of Apple of how they were fucked, and we won't even get started on other startups that have fucked their founders through the VC firms. Startups have been at the mercy of big companies with big money for too long; anything that fixes that balance is a healthy thing.

I love the crypto raise. I believe it honestly allows people with great ideas to have access to funds, while keeping their idea. I believe in a world where only the rich can get richer by controlling everything. This is an amazing step.

Chapter 5 - Bulls and Bears

Trading Crypto is one of the most exciting elements of the whole crypto universe. Because of the intense swings (up and downs) that the market gets, there is a huge amount to be won and lost during these swings.

Trading crypto after it has been sold during a cryptographic sales event is known as secondary market trading.

It is for that reason that some fundamentals have to be remembered here. Yes, you can trade crypto, however, crypto is not 100% designed for trading. So if you are entering the market just for that purpose alone, I would go ahead and suggest you don't. More importantly, if you are planning on trading in the crypto market, you should start in another market first. Wet your feet in something which isn't as volitive, so you get used to the swings which can occur and then take the plunge into the crypto market. Many people who have come from the Foreign Exchange (FX) market have found it easy to play in the crypto market. I believe it is also sensible to measure the style of trading from the FX market to that of the crypto market, although I stress I am not a serious trader.

Trading Utility and Security tokens are very different. Because Security Tokens are registered with some kind of domestic regulatory body under their law, it necessitates that the sale and secondary trading will also be covered by that same law. So, any secondary trading will have to be done through a licensed body which conforms to the laws of that jurisdiction, or which allows the sale to the type of individual where registration has occurred. You should be careful with this. To date, there are

Chapter 5 - Bulls and Bears

no major or successful secondary trading exchanges on the market. This is because to sell such a diverse range of security tokens would be almost impossible. Let's say that for example a security token was sold registered under a Reg S offering in the United States. There would have to be cast iron procedures in place to ensure that such an offering never came into the hands of US Citizens or Residents at any time. Additionally, the same is true for a European Registered Security Token which was done so under the filing of a prospectus. To sell this in the secondary market would require the services of a licensed EU based broker. Then, selling to anyone outside of the EU would also require a broker in that particular location. Based on this we can assume that most Security Tokens are not jurisdictionally agnostic and require registration in one or more locations in order to sell. This creates quite an international mine field for those companies which, with the proposition of selling the tokens after in the secondary market are looking to maximize any kind of raise amount during a crypto raise..

Many argue that this is a contradiction to the crypto space as security tokens are nothing more than a conventional way of raising funds within the international securities framework while just using blockchain technology. Regardless of whatever feeling you have on this, the situation is that in a secondary trading sense, if you are thinking of trading these, you will have to work through the 'traditional' finance world. Although I do fully admit that there are some new model exchanges coming through that are security token only.

It can be said that when it comes to the

Chapter 5 - Bulls and Bears

Security Token market there is a huge amount of regulation which needs to be observed for the secondary sale of tokens, and you should make sure that you are familiar with these wherever you are based. Signing up to a Security Token exchange online (when they exist) may or may not be a strategic and legal way of trading security tokens.

For the rest of this chapter everything we discuss will be focused on the utility token secondary market, which has already grown onto an astronomical size.

For those of you who believe that there is little money to be made in the secondary trading crypto market, the largest exchange on the planet (at the time of writing) Binance, made more money than Deutsche Bank. Think about that for a moment. Within a few years of opening its doors, a financial company is now making more money than a top ten international bank. This should tell you everything you need to know about the volume and the dollar power of cryptocurrency transactions.

Brokers
Brokers, in the crypto sense, are slightly different. This is because they are not licensed individuals trying to connect on the phone to rich people in Connecticut. A broker, in the crypto sense, is a company where individuals can buy crypto directly using fiat currencies. A great example of this in the market place at the moment is Coinbase. They represent a well regulated organization which allows users to buy crypto on their platform via conventional methods such as credit or debit card. They also allow individuals to make withdrawals in the same way.

Although there has been some

Chapter 5 - Bulls and Bears

controversy around them in the past, primarily when they list a new crypto on their website, and through their deployment of different offerings other than their sale & purchase capability, the overall feeling toward the company is good within the industry. There are other companies which will allow you to purchase bitcoin directly; whichever you choose to use it is always worth using a company that is registered in your jurisdiction. In this way, when you need to pay taxes on any profits that you have made trading your crypto, you will be able to download an easily digestible tax form, usually specifically designed for your location. A great reason we also flag Coinbase is that they have a feature to download a trade history which can be uploaded onto many tax preparation websites for years end. Anything that makes life easier is to be seen as a good thing. I must stress here that I have absolutely no affiliation with

Coinbase; I am simply sharing my experience of using them.

Brokers will usually be more regulated than an exchange (which we will cover off in a moment). It is also quite common that Brokers will only sell legacy coins such as Bitcoin or Ethereum (refer back to earlier in the book for the types of Crypto).

Exchanges
Exchanges come in many different forms. Much like the different type of crypto that we see in the market, there are different types of exchanges designed to meet the needs of that market. The idea is that different exchanges will deal in different crypto types. Sometimes more than one type, but as a business choice, usually only one.

As a rule of thumb, there are two

Chapter 5 - Bulls and Bears

different types of exchanges. We can break these down into: rule followers and 'don't ask don't tell'. Those who follow the 'don't ask don't tell' route will often be looking to make trades as easy as possible for those looking to trade utility tokens. More often than not, they will be domiciled in some off shore location, which limits the ownership information for the exchange itself, and asking as few questions as possible. Again, I am a fan of off shore locations for business purposes, however, when it comes to actually dealing with people's transactions, a level of transparency is always a good thing. The objective will be clear, they will be trying to keep transactions at an arm's length. The trades of a 'don't ask don't tell' will not be regulated, there will be no brokers or trading license in place and you can kiss goodbye to your money in the event of a hack or a closure. This is a highly unregulated activity in the 'don't ask don't tell' market. The reason for this highly unregulated activity is quite straight forward: rather than thinking of the process as shady, try and think of it as grey. Remember, the exchanges aren't doing anything illegal, they are just choosing not to be regulated. Given our earlier coverage around crypto, crypto raises and the regulators ever changing view on the market itself, this step is highly surprising.

There are then those who we class as the rule followers. They are trying to offer the service of an exchange in as much of a regulated way as possible, and given the changing international market, this is no easy feet. Many companies will look at locations such as Estonia or Malta that have crypto exchange licenses available for companies. They cost money, and require the companies to comply with KYC and AML checks, but they are a

Chapter 5 - Bulls and Bears

way of showing that the company wants to act in a legitimate way. The businesses will be exactly the same on the surface, and even offer exactly the same service, however one will be conducting business in a very different way to the other.

It is always worth remembering that you will need to check the laws around exchanges in your country. If they are illegal, or the exchange of crypto is forbidden, you will most likely be forced to use a 'don't ask don't tell' exchange in order to place your trades. I point out that this is in no way an endorsement to break the law of wherever you are based, but, as we know, the internet is a nation without borders.

Decentralized versus centralized
On top of the different types of exchanges, there are centralized and decentralized. Peer to peer is the

principal that assumes people trading with each other. Person to person, meaning that the exchange does nothing to do with each transaction. The exchange should be decentralized.

Remember, when it comes to trading in exchanges, you are never actually playing the market. You are playing the bots.

Liquidity and trading volume
Liquidity and trading volume on an exchange are the most important things. The whole concept of an 'exchange' is built around the idea that people want to trade or exchange their crypto with other people. In order for that to work, there has to be many people. The sheer number of people that use Binance, as an example, are why they are so successful. Now yes, there is also the understanding that there are market markers working in the

Chapter 5 - Bulls and Bears

market; we will come onto those shortly. The more people that are trading the more successful the exchange will be, as more people will be placing buy and sell orders on different crypto. Remember, we are only talking about exchanges here. Not brokers. A broker by contrast doesn't really care how many clients it gets, as it is purchasing in the market. Exchanges are people swapping with each other. Brokers are people buying directly from the market. The difference should now be clear. These people looking to exchange with each other make the daily trading volume.

Exchanges make their money by taking a small percentage of each trade that is placed, along with listing fees and promotional income, but that's another story for companies that are looking to be listed on exchanges. We cover that off later in the topic, as it is important to understand how it works especially for companies that are looking to be listed.

Understanding how the trading volume and liquidity is on each exchange is important. This way you can gauge how successful, useful, or important to your trading strategy a particular exchange will be. For example, one crypto may sell or trade very well on a particular exchange. Meaning that the price will be reflected in these trades.

The liquidity is a different story. When a crypto is listed on an exchange, the exchange will take a certain amount of the crypto in order to keep liquidity in the market, this means until there is enough of a market to actually sell these tokens, the exchange can sell them on behalf of a blank party. Of course, as an advantage for the exchange, they will make the money for the back end of the exchange. The

Chapter 5 - Bulls and Bears

downside is that the liquidity of that particular crypto drops. If the amount of crypto held by the exchange is zero for a particular crypto, then we say it has zero liquidity. This means that until someone comes along to buy the crypto at a particular price, the market for that crypto will be flat. There will be no one to buy it. This is where market makers come in.

Market Makers
Market Makers are those who usually work for the company that has issued the crypto itself. Alternatively, they could be appointed by the exchange to be working on behalf of the exchange to ensure liquidity. Their primary role is to ensure that liquidity is kept within the market. They will literally be placing trades for and on behalf of the company, or the exchange; whoever their client is. In placing these trades, both purchase and sale, they keep the

market going or in some cases, make a market.

Arbitrage

Arbitraging the market is an incredibly successful tactic that has been used across different financial markets for a number of years. If deployed properly, it actually acts as one of the most minimum risk trading strategies that can yield massive results very quickly.

The concept of arbitraging is using different exchange prices to buy and sell at low and high prices. As a simple explanation, if Bitcoin is for sale on exchange A with a buy price of $1,000 (we wish) and is for sale on exchange B for a sale price of $1,100, the logical thing to do is buy it at $1,000 and sell it for $1,100. That's a simple example, now imagine across 30 different exchanges if they all have different buy and sell prices for different currencies.

Chapter 5 - Bulls and Bears

The whole trading system can be developed around watching prices, picking up on market movements from one exchange that may be more reactive and taking advantage of that on an exchange which is less reactive. The prices will then be amended to reflect the market change later on which means you can take advantage of this lower or higher price wherever you need.

The real benefit is that the system can be automated. Simple software developed by many traders can be programmed to plug into exchanges, for these to place trades automatically. We discussed this earlier (the bots); however, unlike simple trading bots that monitor and move with the market, these bots are designed to do much more of a specific task. They scan the market generally watching for different buy and sell prices of specific assets.

The Little Book of Crypto

Unlike general trading, these positions are very short, which means that no one is holding onto them for a long period of time. The trades are almost instant, this is, being purchased in one location and automatically sold in another. This high frequency trading style is also married with a stack them small and high mentality. Meaning, the software may only be looking for a small change in price, maybe even a few cents but it will be placing many trades at the same time. The hope is that you will never actually be holding onto the positions for longer than is necessary. The price has been spotted, the system has placed the trade. It should almost be buy, confirm, sell, confirm. Done. Keep in mind that arbitraging prices is less risky than having a fixed position, but trying to do it manually is almost impossible. Much like when we spoke about bots earlier, automated systems will always work better than manual

Chapter 5 - Bulls and Bears

ones, due to the speed at which they operate.

Getting Listed
Getting Listed is an important step for any company that has undertaken a crypto raise or issued their own currency. Getting listing on a major exchange can mean the difference between your token surviving to become a fully fledged utility token, or having it fall by the wayside into the realm of the shit coin.

Getting listed on an exchange is quite a complicated process, one which has a large amount of competition. If you think of the number of good exchanges out there, against how many different types of crypto there are trying to get listed, it is easy to see why there is such competition. Now that we have discussed liquify and trading volume, you should at least have a basic understanding of what makes a good exchange vs a bad one. It is very easy to get listed on a bad exchange, and that should never be frowned upon as part of your strategy. Getting listed on an exchange will take time, as many of them will want to put you through due diligence. And rightly so. That due diligence will be looking at your project, understanding it, and charging you a listing fee. Twinned with a number of tokens for liquidity.

A word of warning here. Never ever trust people who claim to be 'listing agents' or 'sales' from an exchange. Exchanges have a habit of using third party agreements with contractors, who are free to negotiate their own price, and cannot guarantee any actual listing on the exchange. So, when dealing with the exchange, approach the exchange and make sure that you are actually

Chapter 5 - Bulls and Bears

dealing with the company and not a third party.

When looking at what exchanges to get listed on, remember everything is up for negotiation. The exchange will benefit if you have a large user base and you should never forget this. If your crypto is a good one, it will bring more users to the exchange and therefore they will also benefit. So, starting with smaller exchanges can often be a good strategy. It is better to approach a larger exchange, when you have an already active daily trading volume on other exchanges, than actually starting from scratch on their exchange.

Safety on exchanges
Remember, most exchanges (if any) are not insured. They do not carry any kind of financial recognition and are not underwritten by anyone. So, as a logical step, you should not keep masses of

funds in an online exchange. Exchanges, as much as they try to protect their clients, are subject to hacks and malicious attacks. They are also often based in off shore locations (under the 'don't ask don't tell' principle we discussed earlier). So, their ability to simply close their doors as a business, is very much a real one.

Think back to MtGox, which was one of the largest exchanges in the world at the time. This was a company that simply closed their doors over night after being hacked. They lost everything, for themselves and other people. So, when dealing with exchanges, do not get them confused with a typical financial institution that we see today. Treat them as purely an exchange. The best way to mange this risk, is to deposit from a hard wallet (which we will discuss later) onto your online account. Place your trades, and

Chapter 5 - Bulls and Bears

then extract the funds back into your hard wallet. This way, whatever happens to the exchange, you are protected as much as you can be. Build in these protections into whatever trading strategy you chose to implement.

One thing you should also always do, also, is to use more than one protection method for accessing the exchange. Many exchanges will have 2FA built in, or some kind of security method, including phone coding or third party verification; this is is very important. Don't just use any kind of standard access. Protect yourself online with exchange, more so than you do with anything else in your online experience.

The Initial Exchange Offering
We would be totally remiss if we didn't discuss the Initial Exchange Offering at least once in this section. We touched

on them earlier on the crypto raise chapter, in some pretty great detail. However, if you do choose to go down the IEO route (which, in case you didn't pick up my message, I don't suggest) then you should only use one of the top exchanges. The same listing rules apply only greater. Don't pay a heavy fee, require full due diligence on the company doing the raise, ask for details of other raises, and get details on the company that will be doing the raise, including the directors. Full transparency works both ways, so expect to give them all of your data.

On the other hand, if you are on an exchange participating in an IEO, make sure you get all the details around the company doing the IEO. Don't trust what the exchange says, do your own research on the company and find out the exact estimated raise amount expected from the company. Speak

Chapter 5 - Bulls and Bears

with the company doing the raise, find out how much research they have done on the exchange. A well placed IEO on a major exchange will do well. An IEO on a small exchange will only raise a few thousand dollars.

Trading Strategies
When you begin trading, you will want to formulate your own trading strategy. We spoke about arbitrage earlier, which is one trading method used by many. However, you need to work out very early on what your overall strategy is and what type of method works best for you.

Trading strategies are based on a number of key factors, including:
-Value
-Short versus Long
-Risk versus Reward
-Crypto type

Value

The value of your trading style is as it sounds. How much money do you have to lose in the market. The key word is 'lose'. You should never, ever, put more into the market than you can afford to lose. Ever. If you only have $10 a month, then use $10 a month. Do not get greedy and do not get blinded by the possibility of 'winning'. When you put more into your trading account, then you can afford to lose, then you have already lost. Factually. Your trading strategy should build in how much you can put in and what you have to work with. People become obsessed with having to put large sums of funds into their trading account to make it big. That's a stupid idea. The simple fact is that it's numbers, all the way through. If you put $25.00 a month into your trading account, and aim to break even at first, thats $300 per year. Now, if you step up your game, and you try to make

Chapter 5 - Bulls and Bears

12% per year (keeping in mind your bank would give you 0.4% for keeping the same money in a savings account) you just turned that into $336.00. Does it sound stupid? Or like it's not a lot? Well, let's be clear here, leaving it in your savings account at your bank would have made it into around $301.20 compared to your $336.00. So, in that context, who is winning? On a basic trading strategy, this means once a year you get dinner for free.

Short versus Long
The terms short and long refer to how long you are looking to hold onto your crypto. This ties into your value consideration. If you know that you can afford to put $25.00 into your trading account and not need it for six months, then you can base your strategy around a long play. In contrast, if you need access to that money in six weeks, then you know your trading style will be

short.

Thinking back to the different types of crypto, it is common that there will be a trading style aligned with whichever you choose to work with. For example, legacy coins will have a long trading style attached to them. Many are holding bitcoin in the hope that it will skyrocket to $100K+. In order for that to happen, we know it will realistically take years (if it ever does happen). And so, those who are hoping for that are playing long. They are sitting on bitcoin for a long period of time in the hope it will raise. The same is true of other legacy coins such as LiteCoin or Ethereum. In the long trading style you are not concerned with the 'swings' of the market (how much the coin raises and drops on a daily or weekly basis). As long as the chart is heading upward in the long run, you are happy in a long term perspective.

Chapter 5 - Bulls and Bears

Working short on the other hand is a much more explosive and reactive trading style. This is better suited to Utility Tokens. Because the swings on these are usually very high, money can be made (or lost) very quickly. This rapid movement means that you have more of a chance of getting in, making money, getting out. Short term trading is often based around the concept of 'resistance points'. This is where, in a basic sense, you analyze a chart to see if a crypto that is raising has hit a resistance point. If a resistance point has been met, you are looking for a break out or a further retraction. i.e, will it go high or will it go low. The prior movements should give you an indication based on where its likely to go. However, remember that this is a more explosive and quicker trading style, so you may only be looking at a specific crypto for a day or two before you exit your position after making money. There are some people who get in with high volume (large amounts of money) and then sell high. This is known as a 'pump and dump'. They purchase large volumes of a token to make the token value raise, then when it is up, sell it. You should always be on the look out for pump and dumps in the market place, as it is a common way of losing money.

Risk versus Reward
Risk versus Reward is the way in which we can tie all of these decisions that you are going to make together. Your trading style should be a reflection of risk versus reward. Meaning, the more risk you take, the more reward you stand to make. However, the same is true of the reversal, the more reward you chase, the more risk you take. So, this is why the whole concept of a trading style is called a 'strategy'. No one cares about your style.. an idiot

Chapter 5 - Bulls and Bears

with a plan can make more money than a fool with money.

Always respect your risk versus reward ratio.

Stop Loss
A stop loss on a serious exchange can be your best friend. Setting a stop loss means that, essentially, if a crypto drops below a certain point, the system will automatically sell it for you. The concept being that you don't lose more money. Now, try not to think of this in the flat line sense. You should raise your stop loss as the value of the crypto raises. In practice, if you buy a crypto at $1.00 and it raises to $1.10, you should set a stop loss around $1.08 so you maintain your $0.08 profit. As it heads up, you should raise that figure. Without a stop loss, if you are busy or unable to be on the exchange, if the crypto falls to a lower figure, such as $0.90, for

example, then you just lost $0.18 of your position without your stop loss. Learning stop losses on an exchange is the first thing you should incorporate into any trading style. It will help protect the funds that you place into an exchange and learning to use the well can be the difference between success and failure of your strategy.

Hedging your trades
The concept of hedging your trades is quite a unique thing in the crypto world. Without getting too deep into OTC (over the counter) trading styles, that I believe are fundamentally different, it is worth looking at hedging your trades.

Now, this is slightly more complex, and not used by everyone.. There are some online systems that will let you make calls and puts on crypto (usually only the legacy coins). This means you are effectively placing a type of 'bet' as to if

Chapter 5 - Bulls and Bears

the crypto will go up in value or down. Now, that doesn't sound exciting in of itself. However, imagine that you purchase a crypto, with the plan of holding it long. If you also purchase a put on the crypto (betting it will go down in value) then, if the crypto goes up in value, once it passes the value of your put, you have made a profit. If the crypto falls in value, then you did not lost all of the money that you placed into the crypto in the first instance.

In doing this you are totally changing your risk versus reward matrix. What you are doing is making much less of a profit, but also taking much less of a risk. You are literally betting against yourself in case the Crypto drops. This is a great way to minimize your loss potential in the event that you end up entering the market in a much bigger way, should your financial value allow for that.

The Little Book of Crypto

Market News

Your trading style should always encompass research and news monitoring. There's a reason why you walk into major financial companies and they have Bloomberg or some other news outlet on. That's not just for show. We know that a large amount of trading is driven by emotion in the crypto market. That emotion is twinned with the news from companies on how they are performing post raise. Telegram should be your biggest source of news for any project that you are looking at. This includes their issued crypto. So, unlike working in the more public domain, you have the ability to get accurate community based information around a project. This should give you some idea of what is gong to happen in the market as a good community will have moderators based within it telling people when to expect some good

Chapter 5 - Bulls and Bears

news. Of course, at the time of writing the laws around 'inside trading' are non existent within the crypto space, so where as the strict rules would apply for trading in something such as stocks or shares, those tough regulatory restrictions do not apply. And while I would never suggest flat out insider trading, there is much more you can do in terms of asking the company what the plan is and if there is any exciting news coming. The communication is a two way street.

Of course, it goes without saying that there are now a number of specialist 'in industry' publications which promote tangible news within the industry. You should also pay close attention to these, as they will often be well researched, well written articles (as long as the site itself is credible). You can use these news outlets and build them into the trading style you have developed. There is a reason why many fund managers and those in the typical financial world will start the day looking at the market news.

Tax
Remember, as a final note. You will need to keep a record of all of the trades you make depending upon the tax laws where you are based. This may seem like a long task, but if you do not keep a record of what trades you have placed and how much profit or loss you made, then you will not be able to prove it to your tax authority. When looking at exchanges, see what tax documents or reports they prepare in order to make your life easier when it comes to tax season. Failing to report profits made from any source is a serious offense in most countries. There is no point in trying to stay as legal as possible if you are looking to flout tax laws.
Having said that, you should always

Chapter 5 - Bulls and Bears

consider making your trading style more tax effective. Just because you are trading yourself does not necessarily mean that the trades have to be done in your name. A private, off shore, trading firm can do very well if it is using private member funds. The company, if set up properly, would not pay any tax on the profit made and you could be free to withdraw anything you wanted personally, paying the tax on that. Of course, this would depend on your trading value and the tax laws in your home country as to if this was a sensible method for you. It is, however, the stepping stone to owning your own private trading firm/fund which you could use to trade your funds and other, close personal friend and family should your trading style prove effective. Remember, the more money you have in the market the more you can make. However, you should never lose the fundamentals no matter how much you

The Little Book of Crypto

are trading with.

Chapter 6 - Wallets and Mining

Whenever you keep cash on you, you need a wallet. The same is true of crypto. You have to be sensible about storage of your crypto, as recovering it if you lose it can be an impossible situation. To meet the market needs with security, there are a number of different types.

We are going to look at some of the different wallet types that are available to use for your crypto.

Hard Wallets
Hard wallets are often called 'offline' or 'hardware wallets'. They are physical machines which are designed to hold different types of crypto currency. They will often look a little like a USB type device and have a functionality system

on them such as a basic screen or something of that nature.

A hard wallet is a little different to other wallets as it requires to be connected to desktop every time you want to do something with your crypto. It adds some extra layers in, which are ultimately designed to give an enhanced layer of security. The simple fact is that something which is not connected to the internet, cannot be hacked. So, with a hard wallet, all the time when is not connected to your desktop, the only thing you ever have to worry about is losing it.

These are great for people who hold hard sums of crypto, or only trade on long positions. So keeping the crypto offline is a sensible and secure way of maintaining your holdings. Hard wallets also have the advantage of enhanced security both online and offline. Every

Chapter 6 - Wallets and Mining

time you connect the wallet to your desktop you will have to go through a security system before you can take the money off your hard wallet, and onto your desktop. From the desktop you can then upload it onto many trading sites or simply send it to another party as you need.

A hard wallet will always need to be connected to the internet in order to make transactions and move crypto, as all transactions need to be placed on the ledger.

Mobile Wallets
A mobile wallet is essentially a crypto wallet which is built into your smartphone. It is an application which allows you to hold, maintain, and trade your crypto depending on whatever it can do.

Of course, as your smart phone is

always connected to the internet, this poses some danger. However, the added security features which are built into your smartphone are often seen as a fair counterbalance to this risk level.

Nevertheless, the mobile phone wallet is often seen as actually having the most danger. Think how many times you have lost your cell phone or dropped it somewhere you shouldn't have. While usually that presents nothing more than a burden of simply having to get a new phone and move all your contacts and apps across, with a mobile wallet you are literally running the risk of losing your crypto if that phone becomes so damaged that receive is not possible.

Unlike a hard wallet, you can log onto your app and make transactions right form your mobile device. The speed issue is great for those who have more

Chapter 6 - Wallets and Mining

of a trading need while they are on the move.

Naturally, mobile wallets are the ultimate dream for crypto in a spending sense. Payment systems which accept crypto can be used directly from a mobile device. This means that in the future there is nothing stopping you from walking into a store and spending your bitcoin using your mobile phone. Because we need to be connected to the internet, the mobile wallet actually works perfectly for this solution. It has security, internet connection, and the added advantage of having the memory storage to actually keep your crypto. We know that companies such as Samsung are starting to integrate systems into the phones (if the rumors are to be believed).

Mobile wallets also have the application advantage. This means that you can have different wallet types on your mobile device for storing and sending crypto. Having more than one wallet helps you to spread the risk in case the wallet fails or becomes corrupt. Also, not every wallet maybe able to store every type of crypto. Crypto uses different types of chains, so perhaps a wallet that can store Bitcoin based chain crypto cannot store Ethereum based crypto. In reality, this doesn't happen for these two technologies, however its an example of what could be the case for more advanced technology sets.

We then have application transmission. Applications such as WeChat and others are embedding methods by which crypto can be sent between users. There is some argument as to if this will be open, meaning users can send whatever crypto they want, or if the system will only allow you to send

Chapter 6 - Wallets and Mining

their own self created crypto (which will most likely be the case). Either way, it is promising to think that companies which have millions of users are making transmissions possible.

Desktop Wallets
Desktop wallets are a type of software which is installed onto your desktop operating system to allow you to store crypto. These are always needed with a hardware wallet to enable extraction onto an online system.

Desktop wallets are great for those who might want some extra layer of security while still having constant online access with their crypto. An online wallet is more dangerous, but does have speed advantages over a desktop wallet.

Online Wallets
An online wallet is typically what will be given to you when you sign up to an

exchange or third party provider. It is hosted, run, and maintained by a third party meaning that all of your crypto is stored with them.

In terms of safety, this is the worst method of storing your crypto, since you are relying only on the security that is in place with the company which owns the wallet. Additionally, your own security measures are probably not sufficient. Meaning, every time you log in, or use your browser to access the online wallet, you are running the risk of being hacked by a third party from your end. Of course, as we spoke before, there is also the possibility that the company who owns the wallet will not be there tomorrow; these are not like typical financial institutions, they do not carry insurance, and are not backing the crypto in case of loss.

There will be some website security in

Chapter 6 - Wallets and Mining

place with third party online wallets. However, you should always remember that if smart people built it, smart people can hack it.

In terms of speed, these are often seen as the fastest wallets to conduct business. Logging into your online account and then instantly placing trades is a great way to conduct fast trading.

Multi-Signature Wallets
A multi signature wallet is often a hardware wallet (or other) which requires more than one authentication before crypto can be moved out of it. These are great for corporations which may have a large amount of crypto in their possession and have a security concern about one member being able to access all the company holdings on their own.

The Little Book of Crypto

Whichever wallet you chose, you should make sure that it suits your security needs, lifestyle, and trading methods. Having quick access to the internet for some is of paramount importance. If a notification comes to a user that a crypto is spiking, being able to log in and sell that crypto in a specific timeframe can make the difference between making $10,000 and making $100,000. Likewise, if you plan to use your crypto to buy things, then you should base your holding style around that. Standing in a store with your laptop is often not seen as the best way to do any shopping. It goes go without saying also that you should, for the most part, always have more than one wallet, in more than one method, to be able to use crypto in whatever way you need. Spread your use and risk around.

The Crypto Bank
Nowadays the concept of a crypto bank

Chapter 6 - Wallets and Mining

is starting to emerge. The whole idea is not new, as there have been some large companies around that have been offering this service for some time. However, rather than staying objective on this point, I feel I am going to offer my personal opinion.

In a whole system which is designed to be peer to peer (person to person) and decentralized, would we need a bank? The whole birth of crypto came out of not trusting banks or financial institutions. So, why would we turn right back around and start trusting new ones?
I have no doubt that crypto banks will do well, as they are a great bridge between the current financial world and the crypto, so people who are not 100% about taking the jump will want to rely on them. However, in a world where I fail to trust my regular bank which is backed by various government

bodies, I'm not going to start trusting one which is not.

Card Providers
There are now some companies which are allowing users to spend their crypto directly in fiat using a card. I think this is an amazing idea. It is true that spending money in crypto would be better, but for now, not every company is taking it. So, being able to instantly convert your crypto into fiat (or as instant as possibly with the companies help) is an amazing thing. I personally have one of these cards, and it is amazing to think that I have paid for my dinner, using Bitcoin, that I mined at home.

You should look more into card providers if you are looking to spend your crypto on a more daily basis. It's quite a cool thing to have, and an even cooler thing to be able to do. You should, as always, do research into the

Chapter 6 - Wallets and Mining

company before you go giving them over your personal details and crypto. Card providers are not financial institutions, and truth be told it is actually quite easy to spin up a company with a white label card service provision in the system. It is also possible that the provider is not telling the card issuer (such as MasterCard or Visa) or that the whole company is based on Crypto. Remember, earlier we spoke about the old financial world hating the new financial world. Well, card providers are no exception. If the card provider revokes the right of the issuer, then the whole system will stop working over night and you will be unable to use your card.

Remember, when selecting any provider in the space, you should do a huge amount of research. That goes for whatever wallet you want to use or secondary service provider such as card issuer. Developing software to use in the crypto space such as a wallet is easy. Ensuring that it is a company that can last and stay secure is a totally different story. Consequently, do not get drawn in by a flashy website or cool UX interface (this is, how the thing looks). You should worry more about how long the business has been going, where it is based, who owns it, how it operates and what its security features are before you go handing over cash or crypto to them.

Mining
I promised that this book would not go too in depth in a technical sense as to what crypto is, and I stand by that. However, there is a whole massive industry segment known as mining which you have to understand in order to fully appreciate what it is and get a solid overview of the crypto world.

Chapter 6 - Wallets and Mining

Whenever a crypto transaction happens, this is, whenever crypto is sent from one party to another, it is added to a digital ledger. This ledger serves as a record of all of the transactions which have happened over the whole history of the crypto currency. It is literally a list of all of the transactions which have happened since the crypto was created. This ledger is one of the key things which makes crypto so amazing, the whole transaction history is completely open for anyone to see. Right now, you can look at the transactions which are happening on Bitcoin or many other crypto by searching online.

Every crypto will have this ledger. Sometimes these are not open to the public, and we call these private ledgers. There are advantages and disadvantages to both.

The Little Book of Crypto

The purpose of this ledger is to confirm that transactions have happened, and to stop duplication of transactions. It's essentially a security mechanism. It is impossible to fake a transaction, or fake a crypto (meaning, make a bitcoin for example) when the whole system knows exactly where every coin is.

When crypto is sent from one party to another, if that crypto is recorded on a 'mining' based ledger, a few things have to happen before it reaches the receiving party. In a basic sense, the numbers that you see entered into the ledger are made up of a few key things: the sending address, the receiving address, and then a solution to a mathematical formula. There is a little more, but that is all you need to know for now. This solution is the verification that the transaction is real and has happened. Let's put it this way. When

Chapter 6 - Wallets and Mining

you hand over your card at the store, your bank acts as the 'oracle'. This means the system says 'I need this money' and your bank says, 'Ok, here it is'. Then, their internal system verifies that it has gone from your account to the stores account, and you get your stuff. That's why you pay a merchant fee, for that verification that the transaction happened. Now, in crypto this can't happen, because the whole system is decentralized, meaning no one person owns or controls it, so that party can't verify that the transactions have happened.

When the transaction first starts and you hit send, the system will produce the ledger entry, which will be missing one key point. That key section can only be included once a mathematical formula has been solved. This formula is a type of cryptography. Hence, 'Cryptocurrency'. At the back end of this, graphic cards (or other hardware) will solve the equation, and the first one to do it will receive a reward. In bitcoins case, some bitcoin. This is important, as no one would verify transactions simply out of 'love' for the system. The first graphic card to solve the equation gets the reward. This also has the double added effect of stopping people from pressing 'send' on two transactions at the same time.

You should not get mining confused with Nodes. If you have heard this term, then you should know that the nodes are part of the system, and they maintain transaction records. This becomes a little more complex and not something we will cover off in this book, but definitely something you should look into as you learn more about crypto in general.

So, there are literally fields of graphics

Chapter 6 - Wallets and Mining

cards, solving these equations, confirming transactions and receiving bitcoin (or whatever crypto they are working with). We call this mining. When mining first started, the equations were simple, so much that a basic home laptop could verify a transaction on the ledger. However, the system is designed so that as time goes on, these equations become more and more complex. This is because there is not an unlimited amount of Bitcoin (or any currency), and so the reward comes from 'unallocated' bitcoins which remain in the system. This does have an impact on 'transaction time' and creates the argument of why some crypto is better at transactions than others. However, Bitcoin was the original, but as time has gone on and other crypto has been created, some have become faster and faster at this.

These transactions, once solved, are

then marked on the distributed ledger. We refer to it as distributed, as anyone can look at it, check it, verify it and so on. However, the transactions that are marked on it, are not totally open, and there is little to no way of knowing who the two parties are, although you can see the amount and you can confirm that the transaction happened. The parties themselves will get a transaction ID, which means it can be personally checked on the ledger.

Some other crypto does not use a third party verification method. These are self verifying chains, which means that the ledger entries are solved by the systems themselves and not by other parties verifying them. There are mixed emotions about these types of crypto and about whether they really are true 'crypto' in the decentralized sense. While it may have a positive impact on speed, it really is arguable if the

Chapter 6 - Wallets and Mining

currency is decentralized.

Consequently, for verifying chains, there has been a massive industry created around mining. Companies that undertake mining, develop the hardware, software, and other services are all in the crypto space although they may have nothing to do with crypto itself. Take for example Nvidia, one of the world's largest graphics cards manufactures. They never imagined ten years ago that a whole new market would emerge based around crypto for the purpose of mining. They are now one of the biggest players in the crypto space, without even imagining it.

The Energy Issue
The one massive draw back from mining is energy consumption. For those of you familiar with graphics cards and hardware generally, you will know that it generates a lot of heat

while it is being used. With the amount of heat being generated by the hardware, the whole system has to be cooled. Twinning the requirement for cooling and the running of the equipment itself means that energy consumption can be massive. This energy consumption is often seen as one of the major draw backs to the whole crypto system. As more complex equations are generated and more crypto enters the market, the need for miners also becomes greater.

Of course, as we know, for most of the world electricity is not cheap. This means that any mining operation is competing with the cost of electricity in order to run the whole operation 24 hours a day. This has had a global impact on most mining operations being located from countries which have cheap electricity. However, while that cheap electricity may help the

Chapter 6 - Wallets and Mining

mining operation itself, and therefore attract more business to the country, the environmental impact is still the same. Energy is being produced for this whole system and this can have a negative effect on the environment as a whole. We know that if the industry carries on this way, it will cause an energy crisis.

It was estimated that in 2018, within twelve months, energy consumption in the small island nation of Iceland would be used more for crypto mining than to power the homes of the citizens. In an age in where we are struggling to find ways to rely on renewable energy, adding new drains on the power grid is never a good thing.

In the future, it is believed that many mining operations will look to switch to more environmentally friendly methods of sourcing their electricity from renewable sources, which can be seen as a positive step for the industry as a whole. We need to be concerned about our planet and cannot turn our noses up at how much electricity is consumed by the use of crypto.

Chapter 7 - What Next

Now we have had a brief crash course on Cryptocurrency and what it is, but not on how it works in any major depth, and so, the biggest question is: where can you find out more information, and what happens in the future?

The best next step you can take is to understand how crypto really works in a technological sense. The purpose of this book is to teach you how to drive the car (not well, but drive it none the less). Learning how the car works, and how in depth you want to do that, is very much your next step. When you learn more about the technology and the new things that are moving down the pipeline, you will learn more about what particular area of crypto interests you. As a great example, I have a friend who is heavily involved in Mining but does not doTrading at all. In an industry that is so big, you should expect to like some parts of it and dislike others.

I hope that you have found this 'no BS introduction' to be useful to you, so that you can at least understand all of the basic principals of what crypto is and what it does. Learning how it works in a very technical sense will help you with the choices you make and the different types of crypto that you chose to engage with.

I would suggest getting involved in some groups. The crypto world has a massive community spirit, and many people will be happy to talk to you about it. Ask questions, find out what you want to find out. There are truly great bloggers, writers, experts, and information websites out there which will give you impartial and zero bullshit advice.

Chapter 7 - What Next

There are true news websites in the industry, where many thought leaders will write and pass information into the market. In a world of fake news, I truly love that. Most of the time, everything that is published is simply factual. Although, as always, watch out for those 'pay to play' articles, and also, for other law firms paying for publications.

As you grow and learn more about crypto you will also learn more about what the future of the market looks like, and what type of shape it may take. More importantly, as you enter the market you can also have a hand in that. You have seen, I hope, how diverse the legal framework is and how many companies that are trying to do legitimate things are forced to enter a grey area of the legal world simply to survive. It's important to understand that lobbying for change is the only way it will come around.

The Little Book of Crypto

We know that more big players are entering it. We know that banks are now starting to use blockchain and crypto to facilitate transactions; for instance last year Ripple, has partnered with some of the biggest banks on the planet. We also know that JP Morgan were looking at developing their own crypto. As I mentioned before, Samsung are also looking at embedding crypto wallets on their new phones.

More excitingly, and more importantly, we know that more and more people are using crypto. This is huge, as it is only with full adoption of crypto that it will become truly mainstream.

Governments are also taking more notice. China has announced that they are most likely creating their own digital currency. We know that some countries such as Venezuela have already taken

Chapter 7 - What Next

this step (although it hasn't ended well). This can be twinned with big companies that are looking to issue their own crypto; we saw Kodak and are expecting to see Facebook issue their own coins in the next few years. The innovation doesn't stop there, states such as Wyoming in America are flying in the face of the Federal bodies and actually helping companies working in the crypto space.

On top of that, we have seen legacy coins such as Bitcoin classed as a tradable commodity on some locations, meaning that more complex financial contracts are being entered into and it is being seen in the same light as gold and oil in that respect.

The ultimate take away from this book, now you understand crypto in the basic sense, is that it is the future. You need to forget the traditional financial models

The Little Book of Crypto

and forget concepts such as backing, stability, and centralized control. Companies can raise money and keep all their equity, people can pay each other without the need for third parties, and transactions can be done across the globe in a matter of minutes, not days like today's banking model.

If you have any questions, you can reach out to me. I like to consider myself part of the community.

In a world where we see so many people eager to divide us, the concept that I can mine Bitcoin in (for example) Mexico, from a transaction where a guy in France paid a guy in Thailand, and then spend that in a store in downtown NYC is truly mind blowing. Especially when we consider that the whole thing could happen in a matter of minutes. In a world where everything is online and people have no boundaries, we can see

Chapter 7 - What Next

us more and more working together to get things done as we learn that the old method of governance is slow and not good for progress.

You should continue to learn more about crypto, and help spread the word of how impacting it is, in a positive sense. Only once everyone is using it can we truly see some amazing innovation.

The world is a much closer place, more so than it ever has been, and the invention of crypto is only helping the world to get closer and letting more people have control over their hard earned money.

Quick Reference

ICO - Initial Coin Offering, the first time a Crypto is sold directly by a party.

IEO - Initial Exchange Offering, a Crypto being sold via a third party exchange.

STO - Security Token Offering - A Crypto backed by some form of asset.

Airdrop - giving away free tokens

Utility Token - A Crypto which has a true utility

Security Token - A security backed Crypto

Network Token - A Crypto which is needed to let users interact

Shit Coin - A Crypto which no longer has a real use

Off Shore - A domicile which is not part of a 'regular' taxing juridiction

Made in the USA
Columbia, SC
01 October 2025